Dr. Oetker

modern
german
cooking

Dr. Oetker

modern german cooking

Dr. Oetker Verlag

As a starter, the discovery: Everyone can cook

>> We start experimenting with food from the moment our first teeth appear. We soon discover what is "yucky" and what is "yummy". We learn that chocolate on the whole is good but that it's best to forget about spinach. We keep discovering new horizons in the world of food. And we discover our favourite food long before we encounter our first lover.

Nevertheless we still find ourselves rather lost in the kitchen, in awe when we look at the empty cooking utensils. What goes in them and how much, in what combination? How long and at what temperature? Why is it that no one ever said that eating starts with cooking? And the mother who could have helped us is so far away.

Does this mean that the concept of good food is doomed without ever having been given a chance? Not at all. The love of good food starts here. It is much easier than you might think. And it is a source of great pleasure to conjure up some delicious dish with new ideas and a few ingredients, then to share this pleasure with friends. Best of all: everybody can do it and everybody can be good at it – and you will all have fun. That's a promise!

Tasty tidbits

They are quick and easy and they do not cost the earth.

>> You fancy a little snack between meals? Or there's a film on television you do not want to miss and you suddenly feel terribly hungry? There's no need to call for a takeaway pizza or to make do with fast food.

All you need is 30 minutes to prepare these sophisticated snacks. A few simple ingredients and you can start cooking. You are in a hurry? All right, you can use frozen ingredients. And with the time you save on the preparation you can prolong your enjoyment of the food.

Puff pastry pasties with spinach and sheep's milk cheese filling

Look out, puff pastry temptations!

>> No one will be able to resist the seductive smells of these puff pastry pasties. And it won't be long before they give in to temptation. Keep an eye on the culprit – and just make a few more!

For 12 pasties:

1 packet (450 g/1 lb) puff pastry in 6 rectangular sheets

For the filling:

1 tbsp cooking oil

1 onion

½ packet (225 g/8 oz) frozen leaf spinach

salt, pepper from the mill

ground nutmeg

100 g/3½ oz sheep's milk cheese

4 sun-dried tomatoes in oil

For coating:

1 egg

2 tbsp milk

For sprinkling:

40 g/1½ oz finely chopped sheep's milk cheese

Preparation time: **30 minutes**
(excluding defrosting time)

1_ Defrost the puff pastry following the instructions on the packet.

2_ Heat the oil in a pan. Peel the onion, cut into small cubes and sweat lightly. Add the spinach and defrost over low heat. Season with salt, pepper and nutmeg. Cut the sheep's milk cheese and tomatoes into small cubes. Cut each rectangular sheet of puff pastry into two pieces and roll out into small squares with a little flour.

3_ Separate the egg. Whisk the egg white and brush the beaten egg along the edges of the puff pastry squares. Put a little spinach, diced cheese and tomatoes in the middle of each square. Fold the corners of the squares so as to form triangles, Press the edges together with a fork and trim if necessary. Place the pastry triangles on a baking sheet lined with baking parchment.

4_ Whisk the egg yolk with the milk, brush the top of the pasties with this mixture and sprinkle some chopped sheep's milk cheese on top. Bake in the oven, preheated to 200°C/400°F (Gas mark 6), fan-oven 180°C/350°F (Gas mark 4).

Per piece: P: 5 g, F: 13 g, C: 14 g, kJ: 809, kcal: 193

>> *How about a little variation, replacing the spinach and sheep's milk cheese with minced meat?*
Simply heat 1–2 tablespoons of cooking oil in a pan. Add 400 g/14 oz minced meat (half beef, half pork) and fry until brown. Stir in 2 tablespoons of tomato puree and season with salt, pepper and oregano. Add 2–3 finely diced tomatoes or 2–3 tablespoons of tinned chopped tomatoes. Spread the filling on the puff pastry squares, fold into triangles as explained in the recipe above and bake.

Pizza Contadina

Warmest greetings from Greece.

>> Life is full of unanswered questions: where do we come from, where are we going? And: shall I make the pizza dough myself – as explained on the next page? Or shall I buy a ready-made pizza base from the freezer? Whatever you decide to do, it will be delicious.

For 1 person

1 pizza base, home-made

or from the freezer

2–3 tbsp crème fraîche

100 g/3½ oz grated Gouda

5–6 slices spicy salami

3–4 preserved green peppers

some leaves frisée lettuce

100 g/3½ oz sheep's milk

cheese

1–2 tomatoes

pepper from the mill

Preparation time: **15 minutes**

(excluding baking time)

1_ Place the pizza dough on a baking sheet lined with baking parchment and cover with a thin layer of crème fraîche.

2_ Sprinkle grated Gouda on top. Cut the peppers into pieces 1 cm/in long. Distribute the salami and peppers on top of the cheese. Bake in the oven preheated to 220 °C/425 °F (Gas mark 7), fan oven 200 °C/400 °F (Gas mark 6) for 15–20 minutes.

3_ Wash the frisée lettuce, drain well and tear into bite-sized pieces. Crumble the sheep's milk cheese. Wash the tomatoes and cut into quarters. Scoop out the soft flesh and seeds, then cut into small cubes.

4_ Can you smell the delicious smells? If so, take the pizza out of the oven. Now arrange the prepared frisée on top and sprinkle with the sheep's milk cheese and diced tomatoes. Season with pepper and the pizza is ready.

Per serving: P: 66 g, F: 90 g, C: 104 g, kJ: 6333, kcal: 1513

>> ***Variation: Pizza Amore Mio.*** Instead of frisée lettuce and peppers, garnish with 10–12 small capers and 1 small bunch of rocket. Instead of sheep's milk cheese, use 50–100 g/ 2–3½ oz (½–1 cup) Parmesan. And instead of salami, use 3–4 slices of Parma ham to garnish the pizza after baking.

Pizza dough – basic recipe

Home-made is best.

For 2 pizzas:

125 ml/4 f| oz (½ cup) milk

50 g/2 oz (4 tbsp) butter
or margarine

250 g/9 oz (2½ cups) plain
flour

1 packet dried yeast

1 pinch salt

Preparation time: **10 minutes**
(excluding rising time)

1_ Lightly warm the milk in a pan, add the butter or margarine and allow to melt. Sieve the flour into a mixing bowl and stir in the yeast. Now add the milk, butter or margarine mixture to it and season with salt. Mix thoroughly using a hand-held mixer on the lowest setting. Then increase the speed and knead vigorously on the highest setting for about 5 minutes. Cover the dough, put in a warm place and leave to stand for about 15 minutes, after which it should have increased considerably in volume.

2_ Sprinkle the dough and work surface with a little flour to prevent any sticking. Knead again briefly, cut the dough into two and roll out each half to make a circle with a diameter of 30 cm/12 in. Now all you need to do is add the topping.

Per serving: P: 16 g, F: 24 g, C: 96 g, kJ: 2836, kcal: 678

Leek quiche

The queen of quiches.

>> This is a great way to serve leeks. Cooked in a cream sauce in a puff pastry case, this quiche is a perfect dish to satisfy any hunger.

½ packet (225 g/8 oz) frozen
puff pastry

2 small onions

1 large leek

1 carrot

50 g/2 oz (4 tbsp) butter

1 tsp herb salt

½ tsp ground coriander

pepper from the mill

125 ml/4 f| oz (½ cup)
whipping cream

2 eggs

Preparation time: **25 minutes**
(excluding defrosting and
baking time)

1_ Defrost the puff pastry following the instructions on the packet. Peel the onions and cut into small cubes. Wash and prepare the leek, cut it in half lengthways and then into thin slices. Wash and prepare the carrot, peel and grate finely.

2_ Melt the butter in a pan. Add the diced onion, sliced leek and grated carrot and braise lightly. Season with herb salt, coriander and pepper. Whisk the whipping cream with the eggs and mix in. Allow the mixture to thicken a little over low heat.

3_ Arrange the sheets of puff pastry on top of each other but do not knead. Sprinkle a little flour on the work surface and roll out the sheets of puff pastry into a circle with a diameter of about 32 cm/12½ in. Rinse a 26–28 cm/10–11 in springform mould with cold water and do not dry. Arrange the puff pastry sheets in the springform mould so that they hang slightly over the edge. Press the edges lightly.

4_ Arrange the leek mixture in the pastry case. Put the springform mould on the oven shelf and bake for 20 minutes in the oven preheated to 200 °C/400 °F (Gas mark 6), fan oven 180 °C/ 350 °F (Gas mark 4). Place the leek quiche on a cake rack and allow to cool a little. Cut off the projecting edge, remove from the springform mould and serve warm. Irresistible!

Per serving: P: 9 g, F: 37 g, C: 25 g, kJ: 1960, kcal: 469

>> *A little tip:* You may be able to buy frozen puff pastry already made into circular sheets 32 cm/12½ in in diameter.

Potato rissoles

Here only tubers were slaughtered.

For 4–6 people

1 kg/2¼ lb floury potatoes

50 g/2 oz pumpkin seeds

2 small onions

1 clove garlic

5–6 tbsp cooking oil

1 small bunch parsley

salt, pepper from the mill

2 eggs, some flour

breadcrumbs

Preparation time: **30 minutes**
(excluding cooking and
resting time)

1_ Peel the potatoes, rinse them and cook for 20 minutes in salted water. In the meantime, fry the pumpkin seeds in a pan without fat, then chop finely. Peel the onions and garlic, cut into small cubes and braise in the pan with 1 tablespoon of oil. Rinse the parsley, pull the leaves off the stems, chop them up and add to the pan together with the pumpkin seeds.

2_ Drain the potatoes, then briefly return to the heat to steam off and dry. Then mash them thoroughly with a potato masher. Mix together with the onion mixture and season with salt and pepper. Leave to rest for about 20 minutes.

3_ Whisk the eggs. Make the rissoles by shaping the potato mixture into small balls and press them flat. Roll in the flour, the egg and then the breadcrumbs. Heat the rest of the oil in a large pan. Add the rissoles and fry over medium heat for about 5 minutes on each side until golden yellow.

Per serving: P: 9 g, F: 18 g, C: 35 g, kJ: 1428, kcal: 341

Rissoles

Fashion comes and goes but rissoles are always popular.

1 day-old roll

2 onions

5–6 tbsp cooking oil

600 g/1¼ lb minced meat
(half beef, half pork)

1 egg

salt, pepper from the mill

paprika powder

Preparation time: **30 minutes**

1_ Soak the roll in cold water for a few minutes. Peel the onions and chop finely. Heat 1 tablespoon of the oil in a pan and add the diced onions. Sweat for 2–3 minutes until transparent, stirring occasionally.

2_ Squeeze the rolls hard. Mix together with the minced meat, diced onions and egg. Season with salt, pepper and paprika. Moisten your hands and make the rissoles by forming the mixture into small balls.

3_ Heat the rest of the oil in small amounts in the pan. Add the rissoles and fry over medium heat for 5 to 8 minutes. Turn over now and again to make sure they are brown all over.

Per serving: P: 31 g, F: 40 g/1½ oz, C: 8 g, kJ: 2137, kcal: 510

Vegetable baguette rolls

Festive rolls with vegetables.

For 2 people

1 red and 1 yellow sweet

pepper

4 tbsp olive oil

2 sprigs thyme

salt, pepper from the mill

some balsamic vinegar

2 baguette rolls

1 clove garlic

Preparation time: **20 minutes**

1_ Wash the peppers and cut into quarters. Remove the seeds. Heat 2 tablespoons of the oil in a pan, add the peppers and fry until al dente. Rinse the sprigs of thyme, chop coarsely and add to the pan. Season with salt, pepper and a little balsamic vinegar. Remove the vegetables from the pan and leave to cool.

2_ Heat another tablespoon of oil. Cut the baguette in two lengthways and fry the cut surfaces in the hot oil until golden yellow. Peel the clove of garlic and rub the still-hot cut surface with the garlic – the more vigorously you rub the more distance you will have to put between you and other people!

3_ Spread the fried peppers on the bottom half of the baguette, then sprinkle the rest of the oil on top. Put the top half of the baguette back on top. Your delicious baguette is now ready.

Per serving: P: 6 g, F: 21 g, C: 40 g/1½ oz, kJ: 1586, kcal: 379

>> **Little tip:** After spreading the peppers on the bottom halves of the rolls, sprinkle some chopped sheep's milk cheese on them.

Builders' rolls

Hunger knocks off work.

For 2 people

1 carrot

3–4 radishes

2–3 leaves iceberg lettuce

½ bunch rocket

4 slices bacon

2 tbsp olive oil

2 eggs, salt

2 rolls

40 g/1½ oz (3 tbsp) butter

pepper from the mill

Preparation time: **20 minutes**

1_ Wash and prepare the carrot, then peel and grate it. Wash and prepare the radishes and cut into slices. Wash and prepare the iceberg lettuce and cut into strips. Wash and prepare the rocket in the same way and drain thoroughly.

2_ Heat a pan without fat and fry the bacon until crisp. The fat in the bacon will prevent it burning. Remove the bacon and heat the oil in the pan. Break the eggs and slide them gently into the pan next to each other. Sprinkle a little salt on the whites and fry on medium heat for about 4 minutes until the edges turn light brown. Turn the eggs over and fry for 2 minutes more.

3_ Cut the rolls in half. Butter the two halves and place the strips of iceberg lettuce on the bottom halves of the rolls. Then add the fried eggs and bacon and finally the grated carrot, sliced radishes and rocket. Add two or three turns of the peppermill. Put the top back on and your roll is ready. Delicious!

Per serving: P: 15 g, F: 35 g, C: 26 g, kJ: 2001, kcal: 478

Vegetable pancakes

A platter full of vitamins.

>> One of these pancakes is never enough because they are so irresistible – and not only for vegetarians. They are also quick and easy to make. This is how it should be because they are eaten as soon as they are made. All you are left with is a smile.

For 2–3 people

For the dough:

250 g/9 oz (2½ cups) plain flour

4 eggs

1 pinch sugar

1 pinch salt

375 ml/12 fl oz (1½ cups) milk

125 ml/4 fl oz (½ cup) mineral water

For the vegetables:

1 Spanish onion

1 red sweet pepper

7–8 tbsp cooking oil

pepper from the mill

some cress

Preparation time: **30 minutes**

(excluding dough rising time)

1_ Sieve the flour into a mixing bowl and make a hollow in the middle. Beat the eggs with sugar, salt, milk and mineral water using a whisk and pour a little of this mixture into the hollow. Starting from the middle, mix together the egg mixture and flour, then incorporate the egg mixture. But be careful, no lumps please! Leave the pancake mixture to rest for 20 minutes.

2_ Peel the onion and cut the pepper into quarters. Wash and prepare both and cut them into very thin strips. Heat a little of the oil in a pan. Add a few strips of peppers and onions and fry lightly for 2 minutes, then pour a thin layer of pancake mixture on top and cook over medium heat. When the edges have turned golden-yellow, turn over with a cake-slice or wooden spatula and cook the other side until golden yellow.

3_ Cook the rest of the pancakes in the same way, stirring the mixture every time before ladling it into the pan. Garnish the pancakes with cress and serve with green salad if you like.

Per serving: P: 17 g, F: 29 g, C: 54 g, kJ: 2318, kcal: 554

>> **Another idea:** Instead of onion and pepper, you could use spring onions and mushrooms. Delicious served with green salad.

>> *Fancy a little variation? What about apple pancakes,* as shown in the photograph. Prepare the mixture as above but instead of using 1 pinch of sugar, add 1 tablespoon of sugar. Replace the vegetables with 1 kg/2¼ lb sour apples such as Bramleys. Peel the apples, cut into quarters and core, then cut into small, thin slices and divide into portions. Put a little oil in the pan, add 1 portion of sliced apple and fry for 2–3 minutes, pour a thin layer of pancake mixture on top and thicken over medium heat. Loosen the pancake from the pan now and then, cooking as described above. Cook the remaining apples and pancake mixture in the same way. Sprinkle the pancakes with cinnamon sugar, almonds and – if you like – icing sugar.

Salmon wraps

It's all about fish.

>> Wraps can be filled anything you like. Salmon is perfect – its soft meat with delicately sweetish aftertaste, pleasantly contrasting with its smokiness, combines beautifully with vegetables and is a perfect filling for pancakes or tortillas. Are you ready to have a go?

1 red and 1 yellow sweet

pepper

250 g/9 oz rocket

1 box cress

8 soft tortillas

300 g/10 oz crème fraîche

2–3 tbsp horseradish sauce

salt, pepper, sugar

250 g/9 oz sliced smoked

salmon

Preparation time: **30 minutes**

1_ Cut the peppers in half, then remove the stalks and the white membranes. Wash them and cut into thin strips. Pick over the rocket, removing the thick stems, then wash and drain thoroughly. Rinse the cress, pat dry and trim. Warm the tortillas in the oven as instructed on the packet or warm them briefly on both sides in a pan without fat, one after the other.

2_ Mix together the crème fraîche and horseradish, then season with salt, pepper and sugar. Spread half this mixture on the tortillas and garnish with the rocket and cress. Arrange 1–2 slices of salmon on each tortilla, place the strips of peppers on top and pour over the rest of the sauce. Roll up the tortillas tightly, cut diagonally and serve at once, or refrigerate briefly.

Per piece: P: 12 g, F: 18 g, C: 24 g, kJ: 1248, kcal: 299

>> *A little tip:* Serve the tortillas in shallow dishes or wrap the bottom of each tortilla in a napkin. Do not prepare the salmon wraps too long before they will be eaten or they could become soggy.

>> *Variation, the first one: Balkan salad wraps.* To make these, warm 8 tortillas in the oven or briefly one after the other on both sides in a hot pan without fat. Wash and prepare ½ iceberg lettuce, rinse, drain thoroughly and cut into strips. Drain 1 tin of sweetcorn (285 g/10 oz drained weight), peel 2 onions and chop finely. Cut 1 red pepper in half, then remove the stalk, the seeds and the white membranes inside. Wash the peppers and cut into strips. Mix 3 bowls of Balkan salad (each 200 g/7 oz) with the sweetcorn and onions. Place a little iceberg lettuce on each tortilla, garnish with Balkan salad and strips of pepper. Then roll up and cut diagonally.

>> *Variation, the second one: Chicken salad wraps.* To make these, warm 8 tortillas in the oven or briefly one after the other on both sides in a hot pan without fat. Wash and prepare ½ iceberg lettuce, rinse, drain thoroughly and cut into strips. Peel two pears, cut into quarters, core and cut into thin slices. Put a little iceberg lettuce on each tortilla, prepare 3 bowls of chicken salad (200 g/7 oz) and sliced pears. Sprinkle with curry powder and roll up tightly. Cut the tortillas diagonally.

Crisp & Co.
I grill when I want

>> Here we show how flash-fried and grilled food can be prepared without fat. And how to make the sauce too, of course, or a delicious marinade. In the end nothing is better than a decent sauce with... with... with whatever you like: meat, fish, poultry, or cheese. Fried or grilled. In any conceivable combination.

Whether dipped, basted, dunked, soaked or even licked from the plate, the tasty liquid accompaniment is half the pleasure of eating.

Classic oriental marinade

Get closer to the Far East

>> What is the flavour of Europe? Or of Africa or Australia? Nothing comes to mind. But Asia is another matter. No continent has such a distinctive taste as Asia, as this marinade shows.

1 walnut-sized piece ginger

3 cloves garlic

1 tsp red curry paste

grated zest and juice of

1 lemon (untreated, unwaxed)

3 tbsp light soy sauce

1 tbsp sesame oil

2 tbsp runny honey

Preparation time: **10 minutes**

1_ Peel the ginger and cut up finely. Peel the garlic and dice finely. Now stir together the ginger and garlic with the rest of the ingredients with a whisk and mix well.

2_ Put the meat or fish in a shallow dish and pour the marinade over it. Leave the meat to marinate for 1 hour in the case of meat and 30 minutes for fish, turning the meat or fish occasionally.

Enough for 900 g/2 lb beef, lamb, pork, duck or fish

Per serving (with beef): P: 47 g, F: 11 g, C: 5 g, kJ: 1367, kcal: 327

Halloumi marinade

Ever had hallouminations?

1 red chilli pepper

1 clove garlic

2–3 sprigs thyme

salt, pepper from the mill

100 ml/3½ fl oz (½ cup) olive oil

Preparation time: **10 minutes**

1_ Cut the cheese into slices 2 cm/¾ in thick. Then arrange in a shallow dish. Remove the stalks from the chillies and cut into thin rings. Peel the garlic and chop finely. Rinse the thyme, remove the leaves from the stems and chop coarsely.

2_ Sprinkle the chillies, garlic and thyme over the cheese. Season with salt and pepper. Pour a few drops of olive oil over it, then leave to stand for 1 hour.

Enough for 500 g/18 oz halloumi, the Cypriot grilling cheese

Per serving: P: 25 g, F: 46 g, C: 0 g, kJ: 2157, kcal: 515

Mustard marinade

Small grains with a big effect.

1 small onion

1 clove garlic

1–2 sprigs oregano

2 tbsp sharp mustard,

e.g. Dijon mustard

4 tbsp white wine vinegar

4 tbsp olive oil

50 g/2 oz (3/8 cup) ground almonds

salt, pepper from the mill

Preparation time: **10 minutes**

1_ Peel the onion and garlic and chop up finely. Rinse the oregano, pull the leaves off the stems and chop coarsely. Carefully mix together the chopped garlic, onion and oregano with the rest of the ingredients, using a whisk.

2_ Put the fish or meat in a shallow dish and pour the marinade over it. Leave to stand for 1 hour in the case of meat and 30 minutes for fish, turning it occasionally during that time.

Enough for 900 g/2 lb beef, lamb, pork, chicken, veal or white fish

Per serving (with beef): P: 47 g, F: 18 g, C: 1 g, kJ: 1521, kcal: 364

Barbecue sauce

With it everything hots up.

For 6–7 glasses, each

200 ml/7 fl oz (scant cup)

1 Spanish onion

1 small bunch curly-leaved

parsley

300 ml/10 fl oz (1¼ cups)

strong coffee, cold

1 tsp sambal oelek

1 litre/1¾ pints (4½ cups)

tomato ketchup

Preparation time: **20 minutes**

(excluding standing time)

Keeps refrigerated:

about 3 weeks

1_ Peel the onions and cut into small cubes.

2_ Rinse the parsley and pat dry. Remove the leaves from the stems and chop up finely.

3_ Put the coffee in a bowl. Add the chopped onion, parsley, sambal oelek and ketchup. Stir together well.

4_ Put the sauce in jars, close and refrigerate. Leave to stand for a little while.

Per 100 g: P: 2 g, F: 0 g, C: 17 g, kJ: 330, kcal: 79

>> *Another idea:* Barbecue sauce is delicious served with grilled meat and coating spare ribs.

Spicy
tomato and pepper relish

How bold is your tongue?

For 3–4 glasses, each 200

ml/7 fl oz (scant cup)

1 jar preserved peppers

(drained weight 260 g/9 oz)

1 large can peeled tomatoes

(drained weight 800 g/

1 lb 12 oz)

3–4 cloves garlic

1–2 tbsp harissa paste

4 tbsp cold-pressed olive oil

salt

Preparation time: **25 minutes**

(excluding standing time)

Keeps refrigerated:

about 3 weeks

1_ Drain the pepper thoroughly and dice very finely. Drain the tomatoes and chop coarsely. Peel the garlic and press through a garlic press.

2_ Mix together the chopped tomatoes, garlic, harissa and olive oil, season with salt and leave to stand for about 2 hours.

3_ Pour away any excess olive oil if necessary. Pour the relish into jars and close tightly. Refrigerate and allow the relish to stand for 2–3 days.

Per 100 g: P: 1 g, F: 6 g, C: 3 g, kJ: 286, kcal: 68

>> *Tip:* This relish is the ideal accompaniment for any grilled, fried or roast meat or poultry, and with baked, poached, grilled or fried fish.

Spare ribs

Something for everyone to gnaw on.

>> Is soul your thing? Then you will love spare ribs. And even if it is not, you'll still love spare ribs. Spare ribs are soul food, the traditional Afro-American cuisine. So you can either visit the United States to enjoy them or just try this recipe:

1 Spanish onion

1 small bunch soup greens

(carrots, leeks, celery)

10 peppercorns

4 bay leaves

salt

2 kg/4½ lb pork spare ribs

400 ml/14 fl oz (1¾ cups)

home-made barbecue sauce

such as that on pages 26/27

Preparation time: **30 minutes**

(excluding cooking time)

1_ Peel the onions and cut in half. Wash and prepare the carrots, leeks and celery and cut into large chunks. Put the onions, carrots, leeks and celery and spices in a large pan filled with water. Add a little salt, then bring to the boil.

2_ If the ribs are too long, simply cut them in half or into three. Then add them to the boiling water and make sure that they are well covered by the water. Reduce the heat, cover and simmer for 45 to 60 minutes. When the meat comes off the bone easily, they are ready. But be careful: the meat must not fall off the bone into the pan!

3_ Place the spare ribs on a baking sheet, lined with baking parchment. Cook in the oven preheated to 220 °C/425 °F (Gas mark 7), fan oven 200 °C/400 °F (Gas mark 6) for 10–15 minutes until crisp. When they are a lovely golden yellow, remove them from the oven, coat several times with barbecue sauce and serve immediately .

Per serving: P: 45 g, F: 21 g, C: 21 g, kJ: 1918, kcal: 457

>> *Tip:* Serve with roast potatoes from pages 56/57 or potato wedges from pages 52/53. Or with a crisp green salad with a few kidney beans, sweetcorn and cocktail onions.

>> *Another tip:* Spare ribs can also be prepared the day before and stored in the fridge. Cook the next day and coat with barbecue sauce.

Wok work

From pan to plate.

>> The Chinese language has about 87,000 characters. But that is nothing compared with the endless nuances of Chinese cuisine. And most of them can be found in the wok. A patchwork of flavours, ranging from sweet to sour, from spicy to mild. And most importantly, easy.

Anything which can be cut into small pieces will fit in a wok. If you were ever to find a curried sausage in it, enjoy it and give your chopsticks free rein.

Fried vegetables with rice

Delicious disorder.

>> This stir-fried dish does not stand out for its orderly presentation on the table. The ingredients are all mixed up. But do not fret because you will soon find that everything is in the finest order as regards taste.

For the rice:

200 g/7 oz (1 scant cup)
Basmati or other fragrant rice

½ tsp salt

400 ml/14 fl oz (1¾ cups)
water

For the stir-fried vegetables:

200 g/7 oz mangetouts

200 g/7 oz carrots

1 stick celery

2 courgettes

1 red sweet pepper

3–4 cocktail tomatoes

250 g/9 oz mushrooms

3 tbsp cooking oil

200 ml/7 fl oz (scant cup)
vegetable stock

2–3 tbsp light soy sauce

2–3 tbsp sherry

100 g/3½ oz bean sprouts

½ bunch tarragon

1 tsp cornflour

2 tbsp water

salt, pepper from the mill

ground coriander

Preparation time: **45 minutes**

1_ Put the rice and salt in a pan filled with the water. Bring to the boil, cover and simmer over low heat for 15–20 minutes, stirring occasionally.

2_ Meanwhile wash the mangetouts. Then cut each one diagonally into 2–3 pieces. Wash and prepare the carrots and celery, peel the carrots and cut into slices, and cut the celery into strips. Wash the courgettes, cut off the ends, then cut in half lengthways and cut into thin slices.

3_ Cut the peppers in half. Remove the stalks, seeds and white membranes. Then wash and cut into cubes. Wash the cocktail tomatoes and cut in half. Prepare the mushrooms, wipe clean with kitchen paper and cut into slices.

4_ Heat the oil in a wok. Fry the mushrooms for about 2 minutes while stirring, then remove from the pan with a skimming ladle. Now gradually add the carrots, celery, mangetouts, courgettes and peppers to the frying oil in the pan. Brown briefly while stirring quite briskly, then pour in the stock, soy sauce and sherry. Cover and simmer the vegetables for about 5 minutes over low heat.

5_ In the meantime wash the bean sprouts and drain them thoroughly. Rinse the tarragon and pat dry. Put a few leaves aside to garnish and chop up the rest. Add the mushrooms to the vegetables and cook for another 2 minutes, stirring occasionally.

6_ Mix the cornflour with the water, then stir into the boiling vegetable mixture and bring to the boil. Add the bean sprouts and chopped tarragon. Season with salt, pepper and coriander and cook for another minute while stirring. Add the cooked rice to the vegetables in the pan and garnish with the tarragon leaves – delicious!

Per serving: P: 14 g, F: 11 g, C: 55 g, kJ: 1645, kcal: 393

Curried sausage de luxe with prawns
A luxurious combination.

4 frozen king prawns

4 cooked bratwurst sausages

1 spring onion

1 small red chilli pepper

some cooking oil

300 ml/10 fl oz (1¼ cups)
home-made curry sauce
(see below)

curry powder for dusting

Preparation time: **20 minutes**
(excluding defrosting time)

1_ Defrost the prawns. Cut the sausages into slices. Wash and prepare the spring onion and remove the stalk from the chilli. Cut the spring onion and chilli into rings.

2_ Heat a little oil in a wok – or you can use a normal frying pan instead. Add the sliced sausages and brown them well on both sides.

3_ Shell the defrosted prawns. Make a cut along the back of each one and remove the the black thread which is the intestinal tract. Wash the prawns, pat them dry and cut each one into 5 pieces.

4_ Add the pieces of prawns, spring onion and chilli and fry briefly. Reduce the heat and add the curry sauce. Arrange in individual bowls or in a large shallow dish. Sprinkle some curry powder on top and the dish is ready!

Per serving: P: 20 g, F: 30 g, C: 14 g, kJ: 1671, kcal: 399

>> **One more tip:** You don't have any prawns? Shrimps or crayfish will be just as delicious.

Curry sauce
Perfect for curried sausage.

For 7–8 jars, each
200 ml/7 fl oz (scant cup)

600 ml/21 oz (2½ cups) water

1 tbsp curry powder

1 tbsp sugar

1 tsp sweet paprika powder

1 tsp sambal oelek

1 litre/1¾ pints (4½ cups)
tomato ketchup

Preparation time: **25 minutes**

Keeps refrigerated: **1–2 months**

1_ Put the water in a pan, add the curry powder, sugar, paprika and sambal oelek and stir well. Bring the mixture to the boil.

2_ Remove the pan from the oven. Stir in the ketchup and bring briefly to the boil again.

3_ Use the curry sauce immediately. Or put in prepared jars and keep refrigerated.

Per 100 g about: P: 1 g, F: 0 g, C: 16 g, kJ: 317, kcal: 76

>> **A little tip:** Curry sauce is ideal for making curried sausage.

Chinese noodles
with vegetables

Only a holiday in China would be better.

>> Noodles were not invented in China as it is often said, but in Greece. No matter. The Chinese have thrown their incomparable knowledge of spices and delectable ingredients into the wok, stirred it all together and presented us with this sophisticated dish.

200 g/7 oz Chinese instant noodles (precooked)

For the spicy sauce:

2 tbsp light soy sauce

juice of 1 lime

2 tbsp coconut milk

1 tsp curry powder

For the vegetables:

2 carrots, 1 courgette

2 yellow peppers

2 chilli peppers

1 clove garlic

1 hazelnut-sized piece ginger

1–2 sprigs basil

4 tbsp cooking oil

salt, sugar

Preparation time: **45 minutes**

1_ Leave the egg noodles in lukewarm water until they are soft. Then transfer them into a sieve and drain. Meanwhile mix together the soy sauce, lime juice, coconut milk and curry powder in a bowl and stir vigorously.

2_ Peel the carrots, wash and prepare them, cut in half lengthways and then diagonally into thin slices. Wash and prepare the courgette, cut in half lengthways – remove the seeds if you do not like them – and cut into slices, not too thin. Remove the stalks of the peppers as well as the seeds and white membranes. Wash the peppers and cut into strips. Wash the chillies, remove the stalks and cut into rings diagonally. Peel the garlic and ginger and chop finely. Wash the basil and pat dry. Remove the leaves from the stalks and cut into coarse strips.

3_ Heat the oil in the wok. Fry the garlic and ginger briefly. Add the carrots, peppers and courgettes and continue frying for another 3 minutes, stirring constantly. Finally add the chillies and fry for a further 2 minutes.

4_ Add the spicy sauce, bring to the boil and cook until the vegetables are al dente. Season with salt and a generous pinch of sugar and stir in the basil leaves and softened noodles. Serve in individual bowls or a large dish.

Per serving: P: 9 g, F: 13 g, C: 46 g, kJ: 1441, kcal: 342

>> **Tip:** You can also use chard or Chinese cabbage with the chillies. Simply cut into strips and boil briefly in salted water.

Thin strips of beef Chinese-style

Everyone will understand this much Chinese.

400 g/14 oz rump steak

1 walnut-sized piece ginger

3–4 tbsp light soy sauce

1 tsp sambal oelek

1 red sweet pepper

200 g/7 oz mangetouts

200 g/7 oz bean sprouts

1 clove garlic

2 tbsp cooking oil

pepper from the mill

salt

1 pinch sugar

Preparation time: **45 minutes**

1_ Cut the rump steak into thin strips. For the marinade, peel the ginger and chop up very finely. Mix together with the soy sauce and sambal oelek. Stir the marinade into the meat and leave to stand for 20–30 minutes.

2_ Meanwhile cut the pepper in half, remove the seeds and white membranes. Wash and cut into small cubes. Rinse the mangetouts and cut them diagonally. Rinse the bean sprouts in a sieve and leave to drain. Peel the garlic and push through a garlic press.

3_ Heat the oil in a wok. Add the strips of meat together with the marinade and fry briskly, stirring continuously. Now add the pepper, mangetouts and garlic and cook for another 5–8 minutes. Remember to keep stirring. Towards the end, stir in the bean sprouts.

4_ Finally, season everything with pepper, a little salt and sugar. And it's ready! Accompaniment: rice or Chinese noodles.

Per serving: P: 28 g, F: 10 g, C: 11 g, kJ: 1055, kcal: 251

>> **You fancy a change? Sweet and sour pork.** You will need to cut 400 g/14 oz lean pork into cubes. To make the marinade, stir 2 teaspoons cornflour into 2 tablespoons of light soy sauce and 1 tablespoon lemon juice. Leave the meat in the marinade for 20–30 minutes. Peel 3 carrots, wash and prepare them, cut them in half lengthways and then slice them. Wash and prepare 2 sticks of celery and cut into thin strips. Wash and prepare 2–3 spring onions and cut into rings. Grate the rind of 1 organic orange (untreated and unwaxed) using a kitchen grater, then remove all the white pith with a sharp knife. Detach the orange segments and remove the membranes. Rinse 3–4 sprigs of coriander (cilantro), remove the leaves from the stems and chop up. Heat 2 tablespoons oil in the wok. Add the strips of meat with the marinade into the oil and fry, stirring all the time. Now add the carrots, celery and spring onions and fry for 5–8 minutes until cooked, still stirring all the time. Towards the end of the cooking time add the orange segments together with the grated rind and coriander. Season with soy sauce, honey and lemon juice.

Seafood with vegetables in the wok

A delicious seafood pot-pourri.

>> Those who really want to discover the refinements of Oriental cuisine should first get some deep-frozen seafood and combine it with crispy vegetables and a spicy sauce. Quite irresistible!

2 packets (275 g each) frozen seafood mixture, cooked

2 onions

3 cloves garlic

1 courgette

½ bunch celery

½ bunch spring onions

3–4 cocktail tomatoes

4 tbsp cooking oil

100 g/3½ oz glass noodles

200 g/7 oz bean sprouts

salt, pepper from the mill

4 tbsp fish sauce

2 tbsp light soy sauce

2 tsp sugar

Preparation time: **40 minutes**
(excluding defrosting time)

1_ Defrost the seafood mixture. Peel the onions and garlic, then chop finely. Wash the courgette, top and tail, cut in half lengthways, then cut into thin slices. Wash and prepare the celery and spring onions and cut them into thin slices too. Wash the cocktail tomatoes, drain and cut in half.

2_ Heat the oil in the wok. Add the onions, celery and courgette, then fry over high heat. Now add the garlic, tomato halves and spring onions and fry briefly again.

3_ Soak the glass noodles in lukewarm water. Put the seafood in a sieve, rinse under cold water and drain well. Then stir it into the fried vegetables and continue cooking for 3–5 minutes. Rinse the bean sprouts in a sieve under cold water, drain well, add to the vegetable-seafood mixture and braise briefly.

4_ Season with salt, pepper, fish sauce and soy sauce and sugar. Then stir the well-drained glass noodles into the vegetable-seafood mixture. Delicious!

Per serving: P: 23 g, F: 12 g, C: 38 g, kJ: 1509, kcal: 359

>> **Little tip:** Rice and salad are ideal for serving with this seafood and vegetable dish. A little fresh coriander (cilantro), some briefly cooked leeks cut into strips or mangetouts will make it even more delicious. Very important: the oil must be very hot before you start frying.

Fiery love

Or the kitchen remains cold.

>> The main part of the dish may be the meat, fish and poultry but here the true heroes are the potatoes, pasta and good wholesome bread. In this chapter these play the leading roles and reveal the many reasons for their appeal in exciting dramas involving appetite, pleasure and delight. These passionate delicacies will impress everyone as they eat. And you are the stage director.

Pasta and mushrooms
Woodlanders know their way.

>> If you fancy some delicious pasta, ask the gourmets' opinion: most will say mushrooms. Every season has its own kind: chanterelles in summer, ceps in autumn, oyster mushrooms in winter; and ordinary mushrooms are available all year round. Best of all: they are available everywhere.

500 g/18 oz mushrooms in season

1 small onion

1 clove garlic

1 bunch flat-leaved parsley

2 tbsp olive oil

400 g/14 oz rigatoni or other pasta

salt, pepper from the mill

1 tbsp butter

75 g/3 oz (¾ cup) freshly grated Parmesan

Preparation time: **45 minutes**

1_ Clean the mushrooms, rinse briefly and pat dry with kitchen paper. Cut into thin slices. Peel the onion and garlic and chop finely. Rinse the parsley, allow to drain, remove the leaves from the stems and cut into thin strips.

2_ Heat the oil in a pan, add the mushrooms and fry over medium heat for about 10 minutes, stirring now and again. Add the finely chopped onion and garlic and fry lightly for another 10 minutes.

3_ Meanwhile cook the pasta al dente in plenty of salted water, following the instructions on the packet, then drain. Season the mushroom with salt and pepper. Stir in the butter and parsley. Add the noodles to the pan with the mushrooms and stir briefly over high heat. Serve immediately and sprinkle with some freshly grated Parmesan.

Per serving: P: 24 g, F: 18 g, C: 69 g, kJ: 2265, kcal: 541

>> *A tip:* Stir some chopped, roasted walnuts into the pasta – irresistible!

>> *Another delicious variation: Pasta all'arrabbiata* (in the background of the photograph). To make it, cut 100 g/ 3½ oz smoked streaky bacon into thin strips (vegetarians can simply omit the bacon). Heat 1 tablespoon olive oil in a pan, add the bacon and fry until crisp, then remove from the pan. Peel 2 cloves of garlic and chop finely. Drain a can of tomatoes (800 g/1¾ lb) and cut into small cubes. Wash 2 red chillies, cut lengthways, remove the seeds and cut into thin strips. You'd like it a little hotter? Then leave the seeds in. Add the garlic to the remaining oil and brown briefly, then add the tomatoes and chillies and simmer over low heat, stirring regularly. Meanwhile cook 400 g/14 oz farfalle (butterfly-shaped pasta) in plenty of boiling water, following the instructions on the packet, then drain. Season the sauce with salt and add the strips of crisp bacon. Stir the pasta into the sauce in the pan, heat up again and sprinkle with 100 g/3½ oz (1 cup) freshly grated Parmesan or pecorino.

Tomato-ciabatta-lasagne

Stacked high with a difference!

>> You know lasagne? Of course, everyone does. But this one is different. It is not made with pasta and yet it is so Italian that it will be love at first bite. So give in to its charm and let yourself be tempted. Here's how to do it:

1 day-old ciabatta bread

4 tbsp olive oil for drizzling

3 packets (125 g/4½ oz each) mozzarella

5 medium ripe tomatoes

1 clove garlic

1 small bunch basil

salt, pepper from the mill

250 g/9 oz passata or pureed canned tomatoes

100 g/3½ oz (1 cup) grated Parmesan or pizza cheese

Preparation time: **40 minutes**

(excluding baking time)

1_ Cut the bread into thin slices, sprinkle olive oil on both sides and bake on a baking sheet in the oven preheated to 200 °C/400 °F (Gas mark 6), fan oven 180 °C/350 °F (Gas mark 4) until golden brown. Turn over once halfway through the cooking time.

2_ Drain the mozzarella. Wash the tomatoes and remove the stalks. Cut the mozzarella and tomatoes into thin slices. Peel the garlic, cut in half and rub the inside of a large baking dish with them. Wash the basil, pat dry and remove the leaves from the stems.

3_ Arrange half the bread and tomato slices in the baking dish. Put a few basil leaves on top, season with salt and pepper. Arrange the slices of mozzarella, passata and half the grated cheese on top. Arrange the remaining ingredients in a similar order, including the basil leaves. End with the mozzarella and grated cheese.

4_ Cook the lasagne in the oven preheated to 200 °C/400 °F (Gas mark 6), fan oven 180 °C/350 °F (Gas mark 4) for about 30 minutes. Done? Then all you have to do is sprinkle the remaining basil leaves on top and the evening will be a delight.

Per serving: P: 35 g, F: 38 g, C: 43 g, kJ: 2769, kcal: 658

>> *By the way:* You can also include Parma ham or cooked ham in the layers. But in that case be careful with the salt.

Potato puree

Both young and old will go weak at the knees.

>> One of our first experiences with food was probably potato puree. Whether still a child, an adolescent or adult, we all love a good potato puree. But how do you make it nice and fluffy? Try making it like this:

1 kg/2¼ lb floury potatoes

salt

50 g/2 oz (4 tbsp) butter

about 250 ml/8 fl oz (1 cup) milk

ground nutmeg

Preparation time: **35 minutes**

1_ Peel the potatoes, rinse and cut into pieces. Put in a pan, sprinkle a teaspoon of salt on top, add sufficient water to cover and bring to the boil. Cover and cook for 15 minutes until done, then drain. Mash with a potato ricer or masher. Add the butter.

2_ Heat the milk and using a whisk or wooden spoon stir it gradually into the potato mixture.

3_ Continue stirring over low heat until the potato mixture becomes light and airy. Add a little salt and nutmeg. Very important: do not puree the potatoes with a mixer or blender because they would become glutinous!

Per serving: P: 6 g, F: 13 g, C: 32 g, kJ: 1169, kcal: 279

>> *A variation?* You could also use whipping cream instead of milk but in that case leave out the butter. Or replace the butter with 100 g/3½ oz streaky bacon. To do this, cut the bacon into small cubes, fry in a pan until the the fat runs out, then add to the potato puree.

>> *Another variation?* Potato puree with garlic and herbs. To make this, peel and chop 1–2 cloves of garlic. Melt the butter, add the garlic and fry over a low heat for about 5 minutes. Then add the garlic and butter with 2 tablespoons chopped parsley and 1 tablespoon chopped chives.

>> *A third variation:* Potato puree with cheese. To make this, stir 4 tablespoons of grated medium Gouda or Emmental into the puree.

>> *Variation number 4:* Potato with pesto (large photograph). To make this, use green or red pesto – about 100 g/3½ oz – and stir into the finished potato puree. This is particularly delicious with lamb chops.

>> *And the final variation:* Olive puree (small photograph). To make this, stir in 50–75 ml/1½–3 fl oz (3–6 tablespoons) of good olive oil. Drain a small jar of stoned green or black olives, chop finely and stir into the puree. Season with a little pepper. Delicious with ratatouille, see pages 76/77 .

Potato gratin

Nicely sliced!

>> Hot masses are bubbling just beneath the earth's crust. The same is true of the crust of a gratin. Seen in this context, a potato gratin is a world in itself. You don't need to be a scientist to discover this – a healthy appetite will be enough.

1 clove garlic

800 g/1¾ lb firm potatoes

salt, pepper from the mill

ground nutmeg

125 ml/4 fl oz (½ cup) milk

125 ml/4 fl oz (½ cup) whipping cream

2 tbsp grated Parmesan

Preparation time: **30 minutes**

(excluding cooking time)

1_ Peel the clove of garlic, cut in half and rub the inside of a large, shallow gratin dish with it. Alternatively you can use 2 smaller dishes.

2_ Peel the potatoes, rinse, wipe dry and cut into thin slices. Arrange the slices in the prepared dish so that they overlap, like a tiled roof. Then sprinkle with salt, pepper and nutmeg.

3_ Stir the milk and cream together and pour over the potatoes. Sprinkle Parmesan on top. Cook in the oven preheated to 180 °C/350 °F (Gas mark 4), fan oven 160 °C/325 °F (Gas mark 3) for about 45 minutes until golden brown.

Per serving: P: 7 g, F: 14 g, C: 26 g, kJ: 1109, kcal: 265

>> **Another tip:** This gratin is delicious served with meat, fish or vegetable dishes which come without sauce.

>> **A variation?** Instead of milk and cream you can use 250 ml/ 8 fl oz (1 cup) vegetable stock. Stir 2 tablespoons of white wine or crème fraîche into it and pour this over the sliced potatoes. Sprinkle with Parmesan and bake as above.

>> **Another variation?** Potato gratin with mushrooms (photograph on the right). To make this, replace 150 g/5 oz of potatoes with thinly-sliced mushrooms. Arrange alternate layers of potatoes and mushrooms.

>> **Variation 3:** Potato and carrot gratin (photograph on the left). Replace 300 g/10 oz potatoes with thinly-sliced carrots. Arrange the sliced carrots and potatoes with 1 tablespoon of thyme leaves.

Baked potatoes
A handful of fun.

8 fine, medium-sized floury potatoes

olive oil, salt

For the filling:

2 cartons (150 g each) crème fraîche

juice of ½ lemon

2 tbsp chopped chives

salt, pepper from the mill

1 pinch sugar or some honey

Preparation time: **20 minutes** (excluding baking time)

1_ Carefully wash the potatoes, wipe them dry and prick them several times with a fork. Brush with oil and sprinkle with salt. Wrap each potato separately in aluminium foil and seal the ends. Arrange them on a baking sheet and bake in the oven preheated to 200 °C/400 °F (Gas mark 6), fan oven 180 °C/350 °F (Gas mark 4) for 1–1 ½ hours depending on the size.

2_ Now mix the crème fraîche with the lemon juice and chopped chives. Season with salt, pepper and sugar or honey.

3_ Take the baked potatoes out of the oven. Open the aluminium foil and squeeze the potatoes lightly on the sides to make them burst open, then fill with crème fraîche mixture. Serve as it is or with anything that takes your fancy: strips of smoked salmon, a dollop of trout caviare, shrimps or strips of ham.

Per piece: P: 6 g, F: 12 g, C: 32 g, kJ: 1096, kcal: 262

>> *A little tip:* The good old baked potato is too good to serve merely as an accompaniment. Stuffed with your favourite foods, it is a meal in its own right.

Potato wedges with herbs and cocktail tomatoes
Making eating easy.

1.5 kg/3¼ lb fine, large, firm potatoes

1 sprig rosemary or thyme

1 tbsp coarse sea salt

pepper from the mill

6 tbsp olive oil

200 g/7 oz cocktail tomatoes

Preparation time: **15 minutes** (excluding baking time)

1_ Carefully wash the potatoes, then wipe them dry. Cut in half lengthways and then into quarters. Rinse the rosemary or thyme and pat dry. Remove the leaves from the stems and mix them with the potatoes, sea salt, pepper and 5 tablespoons of oil in a bowl.

2_ Line a baking sheet with baking parchment. Arrange the potatoes on it and cook in the oven preheated to 200 °C/ 400 °F (Gas mark 6), fan oven 180 °C/350 °F (Gas mark 4).

3_ After 15–20 minutes sprinkle the rest of the olive oil on the cocktail tomatoes and add them to the potatoes. Bake for 15–20 minutes more until the edges are golden yellow and crisp.

Per serving: P: 8 g, F: 13 g, C: 57 g, kJ: 1617, kcal: 385

Pesto spaghetti
with sheep's milk cheese
In Genoa gourmets are spoilt!

>> Careful! Pesto is a Ligurian speciality which is very addictive. Fresh basil, finely chopped garlic, the aroma of olive oil with the crystalline sweetness of Parmesan. A taste which cannot be described with words – but at the same time is so easy to make. And this is how you make it:

For the pesto spaghetti

400 g/14 oz spaghetti

3–4 cloves garlic

2 bunches fresh basil

1 level tsp salt

150 ml/5 fl oz (5/8 cup) olive oil

50 g/2 oz pine kernels

75 g/3 oz (¾ cup) freshly grated pecorino or Parmesan

For the rest:

2 carrots

1 kohlrabi

2 sticks celery

1 small leek

1 tbsp butter

salt, pepper from the mill

400 g/14 oz sheep's milk cheese in the piece

1–2 tbsp plain flour

2–3 tbsp olive oil

Parmesan

Preparation time: **40 minutes**

1_ Cook the spaghetti al dente in plenty of salted water, following the instructions on the packet. Drain, rinse under hot water and drain again. Meanwhile make the pesto. Peel the clove of garlic, rinse the basil and pat dry. Remove the leaves from the stems and using a hand-blender combine them with salt, oil and pine kernels until the mixture becomes creamy. Then stir in the cheese.

2_ Wash and peel the carrots, then cut diagonally into thick slices. Peel the kohlrabi, cut into quarters and then into pieces. Wash and prepare the celery sticks and leek and cut diagonally into thick slices. Heat the butter in a pan, add the sliced carrots, celery and leek, then fry gently. Season with salt and pepper and add 2–3 tablespoons of water. Cook until al dente.

3_ Meanwhile cut the sheep's milk cheese into 4 pieces of equal size and coat in flour. Pour the oil into the hot pan, add the pieces of cheese and fry until crisp.

4_ Heat the pesto in a pan, add the spaghetti and mix carefully. Turn the spaghetti round a meat fork and arrange it on a plate. Place the sheep's milk cheese next to the pesto-pasta and add the vegetables. Sprinkle with freshly grated Parmesan cheese. Enjoy!

Per serving: P: 42 g, F: 79 g, C: 78 g, kJ: 4994, kcal: 1193

>> ***Turning the spaghetti with a meat fork:*** Turn the fork slowly round and round, so that you get more and more spaghetti onto the fork. On the other hand, if you are in a rush, leave out the cheese and vegetables and only make spaghetti.

Baking sheet roast potatoes
Today the frying pan has a day off.

1 kg/2¼ lb fine, medium-
sized floury potatoes

2 small onions

150 g/5 oz streaky bacon

6 tbsp cooking oil

1 tbsp salt, pepper from the
mill

Preparation time: **20 minutes**
(excluding baking time)

1_ Carefully brush the potatoes under cold water until clean,
wipe dry and cut into slices with the skin on. Peel the onions
and chop up finely. Cut the bacon into small cubes. Put in a
bowl together with the onions, oil and potatoes.

2_ Season with salt and pepper and stir well. Arrange on a baking
sheet lined with baking parchment and roast in the oven
preheated to 220 °C/425 °F (Gas mark 7), fan oven 200 °C/
400 °F (Gas mark 6). After 25 minutes the potatoes will be
golden yellow and the bacon crisp. Remove the baking sheet
from the oven.

Per serving: P: 12 g, F: 16 g, C: 39 g, kJ: 1462, kcal: 349

>> *A tip: This is delicious served with fried egg or 2–3 slices of meat
in aspic with remoulade and green salad.*

>> *Another tip: The bacon can also be left out.*

>> *And yet another tip: Alternatively you can also fry the potatoes.
In this case, boil them first, then peel and cut into slices. Then fry
them with the onions, bacon, salt and pepper in a little clarified
butter in a large pan until golden brown. Turn over carefully now
and again.*

Fried eggs
The most beautiful breakfast.

2 tbsp cooking oil

4 eggs

salt

Preparation time: **10 minutes**

1_ Heat the oil in a large pan. Break the eggs carefully and slide
into the pan.

2_ Sprinkle salt on the egg white. Fry for 3–5 minutes over
medium heat until the white has become firm. Take the fried
egg out of the pan and serve immediately.

Per serving: P: 7 g, F: 11 g, C: 0 g, kJ: 538, kcal: 128

>> *Fancy a variation? Then simply fry 4 slices of bacon and break
the eggs on top. Season with pepper and fry as explained above
until done. Sprinkle some chopped chives on top and serve
immediately.*

Cheese spaetzle

Good honest food.

>> It may not be the most sophisticated dish, but it is both tasty and sustaining. Often this is just what is needed.

250 g/9 oz dried spaetzle

1 onion

20 g (1½ tbsp) butter

200 g/7 oz grated cheese,

e.g. Emmental

salt, pepper from the mill

freshly ground nutmeg

some chives

or spring onions

caramelised onion rings,

about 100 g/3½ oz

Preparation time: **30 minutes**

1_ Cook the spaetzle following the instructions on the packet, drain, rinse under hot water and leave to drain in a colander.

2_ Peel the onion and chop finely. Melt the butter in the pan, add the onion and fry until golden-yellow.

3_ Add the spaetzle, mix carefully with the onion and fry briefly. Add a dash of water to the pan, then stir the cheese into the spaetzle. Season with salt, pepper and nutmeg.

4_ Rinse the chives or spring onions and drain. Cut into thin rings. Arrange the cheese spaetzle on plates, garnish with the caramelised onion rings and sprinkle the chopped chives or spring onions on top. Delicious!

Per serving: P: 21 g, F: 30 g, C: 54 g, kJ: 2412, kcal: 575

>> *A little tip:* You can also fry thin strips of raw ham with the onions which you then stir into the cheese spaetzle.

Potato pancakes

Delicate handiwork.

1 kg/2¼ lb firm potatoes

1 onion

3 eggs

1 level tsp salt

40 g/1½ oz (scant ½ cup)
plain flour

100 ml/3½ fl oz (½ cup)
cooking oil

Preparation time: **45 minutes**

1_ Peel the potatoes and rinse them. Peel the onion. Grate the potatoes and onion coarsely on a grater. Add the eggs, salt and flour, put all the ingredients in a bowl and mix well.

2_ Heat a little oil in a pan. Using a sauce ladle or tablespoon, put the potato mixture in portions into the pan. As soon as they are in the pan, press to flatten and fry on both sides over medium heat until the edges are brown and crisp.

3_ Take the potato pancakes out of the pan and wipe with kitchen paper to absorb excess fat. Serve immediately or keep in a warm place. Continue frying the rest of the potato mixture in the same way.

Per serving: P: 11 g, F: 25 g, C: 38 g, kJ: 1752, kcal: 418

>> **Another tip:** If you replace half the flour with 2–3 tablespoons of oat flakes, the potato pancakes will be even crispier. And they are also great served with apple sauce (small photograph) and a green salad with a vinaigrette dressing (pages 148/149).

>> **A variation:** Potato pancakes with sweetened curd cheese (small photograph). Mix 250 g/9 oz low-fat curd cheese with 125 ml/4 fl oz (½ cup) milk or cream and 40 g/1½ oz (1½ tbsp) sugar. Then stir in 1 sachet Bourbon vanilla sugar or a little grated lemon zest.

>> **Another variation:** Potato pancakes with strips of ham (large photograph). For this recipe: add 50 g/2 oz of thin strips of ham (for instance Parma ham) and 1–2 teaspoons dried marjoram into the dough. Or serve the strips of ham with crème fraîche as a garnish with the potato pancakes.

>> **And another variation:** Potato pancakes with smoked salmon (large photograph). Stir together 1 tub crème fraîche with 2–3 teaspoons creamed horseradish and optionally 1 table-spoon of freshly chopped dill. Top the pancakes with the horseradish and 150 g/5 oz smoked salmon cut into thin slices.

>> **Variation 4:** For tomato mozzarella pancakes, arrange the fried pancakes on a baking sheet lined with baking parchment, garnished with 1–2 tomato slices and 1 slice of mozzarella. Sprinkle with pepper and brown lightly until the cheese becomes runny in the oven at 220 °C/425 °F (Gas mark 7), fan oven 200 °C/400 °F (Gas mark 6). Decorate with basil leaves.

Cannelloni with salmon or spinach-ricotta

Enjoy the delicious filling.

For 2 people

For either filling:

4 sheets lasagne

1 clove garlic

250 g/9 oz passata or pureed

canned tomatoes

salt, pepper from the mill

100 g/3½ oz (1 cup) grated

Parmesan or pizza cheese

For the salmon filling:

500 g/18 oz salmon fillet

without skin or bones

juice of half a lemon

1 small bunch basil

or:

For the spinach-ricotta filling:

½ packet (225 g/8 oz) frozen

leaf spinach

1 carton (200 g/7 oz) ricotta

1 egg yolk

50 g/2 oz (½ cup) freshly

grated Parmesan

ground nutmeg

In addition:

some olive oil for greasing

the souffle dish

100 g/3½ oz fresh grated

Parmesan or pizza cheese

Preparation time: **20 minutes**

(excluding defrosting and

cooking time)

1_ Cook the sheets of lasagne in plenty of salted water with 1 teaspoon oil until al dente, following the instructions on the packet. Drain and cut across diagonally. Meanwhile peel the garlic, chop finely, stir into the passata and season with salt and pepper.

2_ For the salmon filling, rinse the salmon fillets under cold water, pat dry and cut into eight pieces 2 cm/¾ in thick. Season with salt and pepper and a dash of lemon juice. Rinse the basil, pat dry and pull the leaves off the stems. For each of the 8 cannelloni, wrap 1 piece of salmon and 1–2 basil leaves in a halved sheet of lasagne and arrange in a greased soufflé dish.

3_ For the spinach-ricotta filling, defrost the leaf spinach, squeeze to remove as much water as possible and chop coarsely. Mix together the spinach, ricotta, egg yolk and Parmesan and season with salt and pepper and a little nutmeg. For each of the 8 cannelloni, wrap 2 tablespoons of ricotta-spinach mixture in 1 halved sheet of lasagne and arrange in a greased soufflé dish.

4_ Pour the seasoned passata over the rolls of lasagne, sprinkle with Parmesan or pizza cheese and bake on the middle shelf in the oven preheated to 200 °C/400 °F (Gas mark 6), fan oven 180 °C/350 °F (Gas mark 4) for 15-20 minutes until they are golden-brown.

5_ Serve with freshly grated Parmesan, offered separately.

Per serving:
with smoked salmon: P: 67 g, F: 36 g, C: 23 g, kJ: 2905, kcal: 694
with spinach-ricotta: P: 43 g, F: 48 g, C: 24 g, kJ: 2944, kcal: 703

>> *A little tip:* You can also add herbs such as thyme or parsley to the tomato sauce If you like.

>> *Another tip:* If you are making this recipe for 4 people, just double the quantities.

Spaghetti with vegetable Bolognese sauce

Bolognese with a difference – vegetarian style.

1 small onion

1 clove garlic

1 medium carrot

1 stick celery

2 courgettes

2 tomatoes

6 tbsp olive oil

100 ml/3½ fl oz (½ cup) red wine

200 g/7 oz passata or pureed canned tomatoes

1 heaped tsp chopped or dried marjoram or oregano

500 g/18 oz spaghetti

salt, pepper from the mill

50 g/2 oz (½ cup) freshly grated Parmesan

Preparation time: **40 minutes**

1_ Peel the onion and garlic and chop finely. Wash, prepare and peel the carrot. Wash and prepare the celery and cut both of them into very small dice. Wash the courgettes and tomatoes, cut off the ends of the courgettes and cut into very small cubes. Cut the tomatoes into quarters, remove the stalks and the seeds and cut also into very small cubes.

2_ Heat the oil in the pan, add the diced onion and garlic and fry over medium heat until transparent. Add the diced carrots and celery and fry for a further 3–4 minutes. Now add the diced courgettes and tomatoes and fry briefly, then pour in the red wine. Stir in the passata and freshly chopped herbs and simmer over low heat for 15 minutes until the vegetables are soft.

3_ Meanwhile cook the spaghetti in plenty of salted water until al dente, following the instructions of the packet. Drain, rinse under hot water and drain again. Put the spaghetti in individual bowls. Season the finished sauce with salt and pepper and pour over the spaghetti. Sprinkle a little Parmesan on top and garnish with a few marjoram or oregano leaves.

Per serving: P: 22 g, F: 23 g, C: 92 g, kJ: 2884, kcal: 688

>> **The classic variation: Spaghetti Bolognese.** Peel 1 onion and 1 clove of garlic. Wash and prepare 2 carrots and 100 g/3½ oz celeriac and peel both. Chop the ingredients finely. Heat 1 tablespoon of oil in a pan. Add the vegetables and fry over medium heat. Add 250 g/9 oz minced beef, fry until brown, stirring all the time and pressing out any lumps there might be with a fork. Coarsely chop 800 g/1 ¾ lb tinned tomatoes and add together with the juice and 2 tablespoons tomato puree to the pan. Season with salt, pepper and oregano. Bring the sauce to the boil and cook for about 15 minutes over low heat without the lid, stirring now and again. Season to taste with salt and pepper and add a little red wine.

Potato tortilla

Who will have the biggest piece?

>> Nothing can do everything. Except perhaps potatoes. They are really versatile and can be used in so many dishes – such as in this tortilla.

750 g/1 ½ lb potatoes

1 small onion

2–3 cloves garlic

5 sprigs parsley

3 tbsp olive oil

salt, pepper from the mill

4 eggs

250 g/9 oz curd cheese

(40% fat)

1 sweet pepper

Preparation time: **45 minutes**

1_ Peel the potatoes, rinse and cut into small cubes. Peel the onion and cloves of garlic. Chop the onion finely and crush the garlic through a garlic press. Rinse the sprigs of parsley, pull the leaves off the stems and chop finely.

2_ Heat the olive oil in a large ovenproof pan and fry the cubed potatoes all over in the hot oil. Add the finely chopped onion and crushed garlic, fry briefly, cover and cook for 10 minutes. Turn over now and again. Season with salt and pepper and stir in the parsley, keeping a little aside. Now remove the lid and allow to cool.

3_ Separate the egg whites and yolks. Stir the yolks into the curd cheese and mix thoroughly. Beat the egg whites until semi-stiff and stir into the yolk-curd cheese mass. Cut the peppers in half, wash and prepare them, cut into small pieces and add to the potatoes.

4_ Preheat the oven to 220 °C/425 °F (Gas mark 7), fan oven 200 °C/400 °F (Gas mark 6). Put the shelf in the middle of the oven. Pour the curd cheese mixture over the potatoes and stir in the peppers. First fry over medium heat on top of the cooker for 10–15 minutes until the edges begin to thicken slightly. Then put in the oven and bake for 10 minutes. Take the tortillas out of the oven and garnish with the rest of the parsley.

Per serving: P: 17 g, F: 21 g, C: 26 g, kJ: 1545, kcal: 369

>> *A tip:* If you do not have an ovenproof pan, transfer the potatoes into a buttered ovenproof gratin dish after frying. Tortillas are delicious served with crisp rocket salad.

Greens

That's the way to live.

>> Do you fancy a little retinol, a couple of tecopherols or some riboflavin? These are just the vitamins A, E, and B2 and there are many others out there, very healthy but on the face of it not all that exciting.

The head says yes but the stomach would prefer something tastier and more nourishing. But that's enough with either-or! Healthy and delicious need not be contradictory terms. Read about the spring gratin and many the other delicious dishes presented on the following pages!

Caesar salad
The empire lives on. On salad.

1 portion Caesar dressing (see below)

1 iceberg lettuce

some decorative salad leaves:

radicchio or red chicory

4 chicken breast fillets

salt, pepper from the mill

cooking oil for frying

100 g/3 ½ oz (1 cup) freshly grated Parmesan

1 handful cooked croutons

or

cooking oil for frying

4 x 100 g/3½ oz sheep's milk cheese

some plain flour

Preparation time: **30 minutes**

1_ Make the Caesar salad. Wash and prepare the iceberg and mixed leaves, tear into bite-size pieces, wash and drain.

2_ Rinse the chicken breasts under cold water, wipe dry, season with salt and pepper and fry briskly on both sides in a pan with a little oil. Then fry over medium heat for 8–10 minutes until done, turning them over once.

3_ Remove the chicken from the pan, cover and leave to rest for a while. Arrange the mixed salad on 4 plates, stir the dressing into the iceberg salad and put on top of the mixed salad. Sprinkle with the grated Parmesan and garnish with croutons.

4_ If you want to include sheep's milk cheese, coat the slices in flour and fry until crispy on both sides. Cut the chicken breasts and fried slices of cheese in half diagonally and arrange on the salad.

Per serving
(with sheep's milk cheese): P: 30 g, F: 71 g, C: 13 g, kJ: 3363, kcal: 803
(with chicken breast fillet): P: 48 g, F: 52 g, C: 11 g, kJ: 2958, kcal: 707

>> *Another tip:* Fresh baguette is a must with Caesar salad.

Caesar dressing
Ruler of good taste.

For 1 salad:

250 g/9 oz mayonnaise

50 ml /1½ fl oz (3 tbsp) cream

50 ml /1½ fl oz (3 tbsp) milk

1 clove garlic

1–2 tbsp grated Parmesan

1 tbsp white wine vinegar

salt, fresh ground pepper

1_ Mix together the mayonnaise with the cream and milk in a tall mixing beaker. Peel the garlic.

2_ Add the garlic, Parmesan, vinegar, salt and pepper and puree all these ingredients with a hand-held mixer. Season the dressing with salt and pepper, and that's it!

In all: P: 11 g, F: 155 g, C: 17 g, kJ: 6260, kcal: 1496

Preparation time: **10 minutes**

Spring gratin

The oven delivers a sea of colours.

1.5 kg/3¼ lb mixed
vegetables such as kohlrabi,
carrots, broccoli, cauliflower,
green and white asparagus

1 clove garlic

200 ml/7 fl oz (scant cup)
whipping cream

2 eggs

salt, pepper from the mill

ground nutmeg

100 g/3½ oz grated
Emmental

50 g/2 oz (½ cup) freshly
grated Parmesan

1 tbsp chopped parsley

Preparation time: **30 minutes**
(excluding cooking time)

1_ Wash and prepare the kohlrabi and carrots. Cut the kohlrabi into slices and the carrots into chunks. Wash and prepare the broccoli and cauliflower and divide into florets. Peel the asparagus and cut off the ends (with green asparagus only the bottom third needs to be peeled). Cut the asparagus into pieces.

2_ Cook the vegetables for 2–3 minutes in salted water and leave to drain in a colander. Then arrange in a large, greased soufflé dish.

3_ Peel the garlic, squeeze through garlic press or chop finely. Whisk together with the cream and eggs, season with salt. pepper and nutmeg. Then pour over the vegetables. Sprinkle the grated Emmental and Parmesan on top.

4_ Bake in the oven preheated to 190° C/375 °F (Gas mark 5), fan oven 170° C/340° F (Gas mark 3½) for 20–30 minutes until done. Sprinkle freshly chopped parsley on top.

Per serving: P: 19 g, F: 32 g, C: 8 g, kJ: 1676, kcal: 401

>> **Another idea:** *You can also use other vegetables depending on the season.*

Mother's potato salad

Only at home does it taste this good.

>> Those checking out of Mother's Hotel will probably have just moved in on their own. They are missing a cuisine which no restaurant can offer them. So when you feel homesick, this is the perfect comfort food:

1 kg/2¼ lb firm potatoes

1 onion

1 small bunch spring onions

1 bunch radishes

1 small jar small pickled gherkins

For the sauce:

6 tbsp mayonnaise

2 tsp medium mustard

300 g/10 oz crème fraîche

salt, pepper from the mill

sugar or honey

gherkin water

Preparation time: **50 minutes** (excluding cooling time)

1_ Wash the potatoes and bring to the boil in salted water. Cook for 25–30 minutes until done. Drain, leave to cool, then peel and cut into slices. Peel the onion and chop finely. Wash and prepare the spring onions and cut into rings. Wash and trim the radishes and cut into quarters. Cut the gherkins into slices (keep some the gherkin water from the jar aside).

2_ To make the sauce, mix together the mayonnaise, mustard and crème fraîche. Season with salt and pepper and add a little sugar or honey. Add all the ingredients to the sauce, stir well and put the salad in the refrigerator for 30 minutes. Season the salad again with salt, pepper and sugar or honey just before serving.

Per serving: P: 8 g, F: 39 g, C: 46 g, kJ: 2393, kcal: 573

>> *In addition:* Some of the potatoes can be replaced by other varieties of potato such as purple potatoes, sweet potatoes or Jerusalem artichokes.

>> *You can make the salad lighter* by replacing the crème fraîche with yoghurt.

>> *A variation? Potato salad with pesto* as shown in the small photograph. To make this, cook 1 kg/2¼ lb of small new potatoes with their skins on. Then cut in half. Drain 200 g/7 oz sun-dried tomatoes from a jar. Put in a bowl with 100 g/3½ oz green pesto and the juice of 1–2 lemons. Mix well. Season with salt and pepper, then add a little olive oil. Cover and leave to stand for 1 hour but not in the refrigerator. By the way: the pesto potato salad is delicious with dishes based on Mediterranean fish.

Ratatouille

A visit to Provence.

>> Ratatouille is a French word meaning a mixture of vegetables – a real cocktail of vitamins. It is also delicious served with meat or fish. But is also perfect served with a simple baguette and a glass of red wine.

1 Spanish onion

2 cloves garlic

1 each red, yellow and green

sweet peppers

1 aubergine

2 courgettes

1 small sprig rosemary

1 small bunch thyme

4 tbsp olive oil

salt, pepper from the mill

1 can peeled tomatoes

(net weight 800 g/1¾ lb)

Preparation time: **40 minutes**

1_ Peel the onion and garlic and chop finely. Cut the peppers in half, remove the stalks and seeds as well as the white membranes inside. Wash the peppers and cut into cubes.

2_ Wash the aubergine and courgettes, cut off the ends and cut both into small cubes. Rinse the rosemary and thyme, pat dry, pull the leaves off the stems and chop coarsely.

3_ Heat a little olive oil in a wide saucepan or sauté pan, add the cubed aubergines and courgettes separately and fry. Season with salt and pepper and put aside. Pour the rest of the olive oil in the pan, add the onion and peppers and fry. Season with salt and pepper. Add the garlic and fry.

4_ Open the can of tomatoes and pour some of the juice into the vegetables. Puree the rest of the tomatoes and juice with a hand-held blender and stir into the vegetables. Simmer for 10–15 minutes over low heat, stirring now and again.

5_ When the sauce has slightly reduced and thickened, add the chopped herbs together with the fried aubergines and courgettes. Stir carefully and season with salt and pepper.

Per serving: P: 6 g, F: 11 g, C: 14 g, kJ: 805, kcal: 191

>> *A delicious tip: Put in the refrigerator to cool and serve with cold fish or cold roast meats. Ratatouille can also be coarsely chopped and served on grilled baguettes as an appetiser. Or put it in shallow individual ramekins, cover with a little goat's cheese or sheep's milk cheese and brown under the grill.*

Rocket salad

Go for green.

1 bowl or 2 bunches rocket

2 tomatoes

3–4 tbsp balsamic vinegar

1 tbsp runny honey

salt, pepper from the mill

6 tbsp olive oil

12 slices Parma or

Serrano ham

100 g/3½ oz Parmesan in the

piece

Preparation time: **20 minutes**

1_ Wash the rocket and drain thoroughly. Wash the tomatoes, cut them into quarters, remove the seeds and cut into cubes. Season with honey, salt and pepper and whisk in the oil. Arrange the rocket on individual plates or one larger serving plate and sprinkle the dressing on top.

2_ Arrange the ham on top of the salad, shave some Parmesan on top with a potato peeler and garnish with the cubed tomatoes. A few turns of the peppermill and your salad is ready!

Per serving: P: 16 g, F: 25 g, C: 6 g, kJ: 1316, kcal: 314

>> **Crispy tip:** Serve with freshly baked baguette.

>> *Variation: Rocket salad with strips of chicken breasts.* Wash 400 g/14 oz of chicken breasts under cold water, wipe dry and cut into thin strips. Mix together 1 tablespoon balsamic vinegar, 1 tablespoon liquid honey, salt and pepper and stir into the strips of chicken breast. Lightly roast 2 tablespoons of pine kernels in a pan without fat and remove from the pan. Then heat 2 tablespoons olive oil in the pan and fry the marinated strips of chicken breasts for 3–4 minutes, stirring occasionally. Prepare the salad as described in the recipe above but without the ham. Arrange the strips of chicken breasts and pine kernels on the salad and enjoy!

Salad with roast oyster mushrooms

Strictly vegetarian but with a meaty flavour!

250 g/9 oz mixed leaves, e.g.
oak leaf, lollo rosso, frisée,
lamb's lettuce, radicchio

6 tbsp olive oil

3–4 tbsp sherry vinegar

1 tbsp runny honey

salt, pepper from the mill

For the mushrooms:

500 g/18 oz oyster
mushrooms

8 tbsp olive oil

8 tbsp balsamic-vinegar

1 tbsp runny honey

Preparation time: **30 minutes**

1_ Wash and prepare the lettuce and leave to drain. Stir together the oil, vinegar, honey, salt and pepper.

2_ Wipe the oyster mushrooms clean, cut off the hard stems and cut into pieces. Line a baking sheet with baking parchment and arrange the oyster mushrooms on it. Season with salt and pepper and sprinkle with olive oil.

3_ Roast the oyster mushrooms for about 10 minutes in the oven preheated to 250 °C/480 °F (Gas mark 9), fan oven 230 °C/450 °F (Gas mark 8). They should be crisp in many places.

4_ Take the baking sheet out of the oven, sprinkle some balsamic vinegar over the mushrooms and drizzle a little honey on top.

5_ Stir the sauce into the salad, then arrange on individual plates or a serving dish. Put the oyster mushrooms on top and serve immediately.

Per serving: P: 4 g, F: 27 g, C: 8 g, kJ: 1239, kcal: 296

>> **This tastes even better:** Make the salad even more interesting by adding cocktail tomatoes, cut in half, and garnish with croutons. Or serve it with warm goat's cheese on a slice of French bread, warmed up in the still hot oven. Indispensable: a crisp baguette.

Summer salad with strips of chicken breast

Which came first: the chicken or the salad?

>> You can enjoy spring all year round with crispy vitamins and tender chicken: delicious and light. And it is not only good for its nutritional value, because such a summer salad is also quick and easy to make.

1 small head lollo rosso

1 small head lollo bionda

1 handful lamb's lettuce

2 spring onions

½ red and ½ yellow sweet peppers

2 chicken breast fillets (150 g/5 oz each)

4 tbsp cooking oil

40 g/1½ oz (3 tbsp) herb butter (e.g. from page 147)

salt, pepper from the mill

50 ml /1½ fl oz (3 tbsp) chicken stock

3 tbsp white wine vinegar

Preparation time: **25 minutes**

1_ Wash and prepare the lettuce, then tear into bite-size pieces. Wash thoroughly and leave to drain. Wash and prepare the spring onions and slice diagonally into rings. Wash and prepare the peppers and cut into strips. Wash the chicken fillets thoroughly, wipe dry, and cut the meat across the grain into thin slices as thick as the slices of peppers and spring onions.

2_ Heat a little of the oil in the pan. Add the strips of chicken and fry briefly, then add the spring onions, peppers and herb butter. Fry for 2–3 minutes and remove from the pan. Only season now with salt and freshly ground pepper and keep in a warm place.

3_ For the sauce, add the stock to the cooking residue in the pan and season with wine vinegar, salt and pepper. Then whisk in the rest of the oil. Arrange the salad with strips of chicken on a serving dish or in a salad bowl and sprinkle the lukewarm sauce on top.

Per serving: P: 20 g, F: 19 g, C: 4 g, kJ: 1158, kcal: 277

Pleasures by the spoonful

From the depth of the bowl.

>> No slowing down by having to bite. No distracting chewing. Just simply delicious soups, thick or thin, clear or creamy. Intense moments of delight for your taste buds. delivered in a spoon.

Chilli without carne

No heat, no meat.

>> Whenever the word "chilli" appears, gustatory nerves go under cover, because this respectable Mexican dish knows no mercy. But here is an alternative without heat or meat:

1 Spanish onion

2 cloves garlic

1 thick carrot

1 each red, yellow and green sweet pepper

1 small aubergine

1 courgette

2–3 tbsp olive oil

1 can peeled tomatoes (drained weight 800 g/1¾ lb)

2 small cans kidney beans (drained weight 250 g/9 oz each)

1 small sprig rosemary

1 small bunch thyme

salt, pepper from the mill

Preparation time: **60 minutes**

1_ Peel the onion and garlic and chop finely. Peel the carrots. Cut the peppers in half, remove the stalks and seeds as well as the white membranes and wash. Wash the aubergine and courgettes and cut off the ends. Now cut all these vegetables into small cubes.

2_ First fry the diced onion and carrots lightly in olive oil in a pan over not too high a heat. Then add the peppers and garlic and fry. Finally add the aubergine and courgette and fry.

3_ Puree the peeled tomatoes together with the juice and add to the pan together with the kidney beans. Bring everything to the boil, cover and simmer over low heat for 30–40 minutes. Stir occasionally.

4_ Rinse the rosemary and thyme, pat dry, remove the leaves from the stems and chop. Add to the pan 10 minutes before the end of the cooking time. Cook until done and season with salt and a generous amount of pepper.

Per serving: P: 13 g, F: 8 g, C: 25 g, kJ: 980, kcal: 234

>> **Little tip:** You can also make this dish spicy with chopped chillies and a few dashes of Tabasco. Leave to stand in the refrigerator overnight and your chilli will taste twice as nice. Serve with noodles or potatoes cut into cubes. Or serve simply with pitta bread. A small dollop of crème fraîche on the hot chilli will counteract the heat.

>> **Variation: Chilli con carne.** Prepare everything as explained above but fry 300 g/10 oz minced beef (or mixed minced meat) together with the diced onion and carrot and season generously with chilli powder.

Herb soup

All good things from the garden.

1 small bunch each rocket, chervil, basil and parsley

1 small box cress

1 onion, 1 tbsp butter

salt, pepper from the mill

400 ml/14 fl oz (1¾ cups) vegetable stock

125 ml/4 fl oz (½ cup) cream or 125 g/4½ oz crème fraîche

ground nutmeg

Preparation time: **40 minutes**

1_ Wash the rocket and herbs and pat dry. Pull the chervil, basil and parsley leaves off the stems and chop up the chervil and parsley stems. Do not use the woody stems of the basil. Cut off the cress with scissors but put a little aside for garnish. Peel the onion and cut into cubes.

2_ Melt the butter in a pan, add the chopped stems and onion and fry. Season with salt and pepper. Pour in the stock. Then bring to the boil and simmer for 15 minutes.

3_ Finely chop the herbs without the stems and cut the rocket into strips. Now add the cream or crème fraîche, herbs, cress and rocket to the soup. Puree with a hand-held blender until completely smooth. Warm briefly but do not boil.

4_ Season with salt, pepper and nutmeg. Garnish with cress and serve in soup bowls or plates,.

Per serving: P: 2 g, F: 14 g, C: 3 g, kJ: 607, kcal: 146

Carrot and ginger soup with prawns

A finder's reward in every bowl.

500 g/18 oz carrots, 1 onion

1 walnut-sized piece ginger

50 g/2 oz (4 tbsp) butter

1 pinch sugar

80 ml/3 fl oz orange juice

800 ml/28 fl oz (3½ cups) vegetable stock

salt, pepper from the mill

4 king prawns (fresh or frozen)

1 tbsp cooking oil

2 tbsp lemon juice

some sweet-and-sour chilli sauce

100 g/3½ oz crème fraîche

Preparation time: **45 minutes**

1_ Wash and prepare the carrots and peel; peel the onion and chop both coarsely. Peel the ginger and slice finely. Melt the butter in a pan, add the chopped vegetables and the ginger and fry with a little sugar. Add the orange juice and stock. Bring to the boil, cover and simmer for 15 minutes until done.

2_ Cut the prawns almost completely open lengthways, open up and remove the intestinal tract – that is, the black thread. Fry them briskly on the inside in a little oil in a hot pan. Season with salt and pepper. Pour the lemon juice into the pan; cover and keep in a warm place.

3_ Now stir the crème fraîche and chilli sauce into the soup and puree with a hand-held blender until completely smooth. Adjust the seasoning with a more little salt and pepper and add the prawns to the soup. Bon appetit!

Per serving: P: 5 g, F: 17 g, C: 8 g, kJ: 915, kcal: 219

Red Thai curry with chicken

The cook sees red.

>> A flight to Asia lasts about 12 hours. But if you fly with this bird you will be able to enjoy this Thai delight much quicker.

4 chicken breast fillets
(about 140 g/5 oz each)

2 carrots

1 sweet potato

1 half celeriac

2 tbsp cooking oil

2 tbsp red curry paste

1 large can pineapple chunks
(drained weight 500 g/18 oz)

1 stem lemon grass

500 ml/17 fl oz (2¼ cups)
coconut milk

500 ml/17 fl oz (2¼ cups)
chicken or vegetable stock

5 lime leaves

2 fresh red chilli peppers

some fish sauce

1 small bunch basil

salt

Preparation time: **60 minutes**

1_ Rinse the chicken fillets, pat dry and cut into thin strips. Wash and prepare the carrots, sweet potato and celery; peel and chop into small cubes. Heat the oil in a pan, add the curry paste and fry briefly. Now add the chicken and fry briefly; then add the pineapple chunks and juice. Finally stir in the chopped vegetables and heat up.

2_ Crush the lemon grass on the work top with a small, heavy pan so that the aroma can develop fully. Add the lemon grass, the coconut milk, stock and lime leaves and bring to the boil. Remove the stalks of the chillies, cut into rings and add to the curry. Season with fish sauce and simmer for 25–30 minutes.

3_ Rinse the basil, pat dry, pull the leaves off the stems and add to the curry 5 minutes before the end of the cooking. Season with salt and fish sauce. Perfect for serving in bowls or deep soup plates.

Per serving: P: 38 g, F: 31 g, C: 54 g, kJ: 2676, kcal: 642

>> *Little tip:* Delicious served with Basmati rice.

>> *Fancy a variation on the theme? Yellow beef curry.* To make this dish: cut 500 g/18 oz lean beef fillet or rump steak into thin strips. Wash 1 green chilli and cut diagonally into rings. Drain 100 g/3½ oz bamboo shoots (from a tin or jar) thoroughly. Rinse a small bunch of basil, pat dry and pull the leaves off the stems. Heat 400 ml/14 fl oz (1 ¾ cups) coconut milk in a wok or pan and stir in 2 teaspoons yellow curry paste and 2 teaspoons turmeric. Now add the meat, two-thirds of the basil leaves, rings of chillies, bamboo shoots and a little sugar. Simmer everything for 8–10 minutes. Season the sauce again with fish sauce and salt before serving and sprinkle the rest of the basil leaves on top.

Chicken broth

It's quite clear.

>> Are you lovesick? Do you have a cold? Chicken broth is the answer to almost any ailment. But even if you are not suffering from anything, you will still enjoy this most classic of soups.

1 boiling fowl (about
1.5 kg/3¼ lb)

1 tbsp salt

1 bunch soup greens (carrots, carrots, celery)

1 clove garlic

10 peppercorns

2 bay leaves

1 small bunch parsley and thyme

Preparation time: **30 minutes**

1_ Wash the chicken thoroughly inside and out. If necessary, remove the innards. Put the chicken in a large pan and sprinkle salt on top.

2_ Wash and prepare the vegetables, then peel and chop coarsely. Add the condiments and peeled, coarsely chopped garlic. Cover with water and simmer without lid for 2–3 hours, adding more water during the cooking process if necessary. Remove any foam which may appear on top with a skimming ladle or large tablespoon.

3_ Add the parsley and thyme 15 minutes before the end of the cooking time and leave to draw. Then take everything out and strain the broth through a fine sieve.

4_ Remove the skin of the chicken and take the meat off the bones. You can use it in soups, salads or sandwiches.

Per serving: P: 22 g, F: 17 g, C: 1 g, kJ: 1025, kcal: 245

>> *A few tips:* Chicken broth is an ideal stock for making risotto, but with the addition of fresh herbs and slices and strips of vegetables, this simple vegetable broth can be turned into a delicious, colourful soup (photograph). A dash of port or sherry will not go amiss. If you cut the chicken breasts into thin slices and sprinkle them with a little vinaigrette, it makes a nice little starter. Finally you can very easily freeze the rest of the broth.

>> *This is how professionals do it:* Wash a large onion but do not peel; cut it in half and brown in a pan without fat with the cut surface facing down. You can even let the cut surfaces go slightly black. The taste and colour of the broth will become even more intense. Then add to the pan, cook with the rest of the ingredients and take out at the end with the rest of the vegetables.

Potato and coconut soup with lemon grass

Newly from the Caribbean.

5 stems lemon grass

200 g/7 oz potatoes

1 walnut-sized piece ginger

1 tbsp olive oil or sesame oil

100 ml/3½ fl oz (½ cup)
white wine

400 ml/14 fl oz (1¾ cups)
chicken stock

400 ml/14 fl oz (1¾ cups)
coconut milk

4 mangetouts

1 small chicken breast fillet

1 tbsp olive oil, salt, pepper

1 dash lemon juice

Preparation time: **40 minutes**

1_ Cut the lemon grass stems into pieces. Peel the potatoes, rinse and cut into cubes. Peel the ginger and cut into thin slices. Put all the ingredients together with the pieces of lemon grass and fry briefly in a little oil in a pan. Pour in the white wine, chicken stock and coconut milk. Cover and cook the potatoes over low heat for about 20 minutes.

2_ Meanwhile blanch the mangetouts in boiling salted water for 1 minute, drain and rinse under cold water.

3_ Rinse the chicken fillets, wipe dry, cut into cubes and fry all over in a little oil in a pan. Season with salt and pepper and a dash of lemon juice. Thread one chicken cube and one mangetout onto each skewer.

4_ Remove the pieces of lemon grass from the soup. Puree the soup until completely smooth with a hand-held blender, season with salt and pepper and garnish with the skewers. And it's ready!

Per serving: P: 10 g, F: 20 g, C: 9 g, kJ: 1156, kcal: 279

Sweet potato soup with mascarpone and hazelnuts

Funny lumps to spoon out.

2 tbsp butter, 2 tbsp cooking oil

1 onion, 1 clove garlic

500 g/18 oz sweet potato

1 walnut-sized piece ginger

750 ml/1¼ pints (3½ cups)
vegetable stock

100 g/3½ oz hazelnut kernels

250 g/9 oz mascarpone

salt, pepper from the mill

Preparation time: **50 minutes**

1_ Melt the butter together with the oil in a large pan. Peel the onion and garlic, chop, add both to the pan and fry.

2_ Peel the potatoes, rinse and cut into cubes. Peel the ginger and chop finely. Add both to the pan, fry briefly and add the stock. Bring to the boil, cover and simmer for 30 minutes.

3_ Lightly toast the hazelnuts in a pan without fat, allow to cool and chop coarsely. Puree the soup a little with a hand-held blender – some people like it very smooth while others prefer it with a few pieces left. Stir in the mascarpone and warm up briefly. Season with a little more salt and pepper and sprinkle the hazelnuts on top.

Per serving: P: 6 g, F: 47 g, C: 29 g, kJ: 2385, kcal: 569

Yellow lentil soup
with yoghurt

Discover your new favourite colour.

>>   This lentil soup is not only healthy, it is also absolutely delicious. Just have a look
at the recipe:

1 small onion

1 clove garlic

2 tbsp cooking oil

1 pinch cumin

1 pinch ground coriander

1 pinch cayenne pepper

200 g/7 oz sun-dried yellow

or red lentils

600 ml/21 oz (2½ cups)

vegetable stock

1 small can sweetcorn

(drained weight 140 g/5 oz)

1 tbsp raisins or currants

soaked in water

200 g/7 oz yoghurt

1 dash cream

salt, pepper from the mill

1 dash lemon juice

1 small bunch flat-leaved

parsley

Preparation time: **45 minutes**

1_   Peel the onion and garlic and chop up finely. Add the chopped
onion in a pan with some oil and fry. Add the garlic after
about 5 minutes and fry for a further 5 minutes. Add the
spices and stir well.

2_   Add the lentils and vegetable stock, stir well and bring
everything to the boil. Cover and simmer lightly for
30 minutes, stirring now and again.

3_   Now add the corn, raisins or currants, yoghurt and cream. Stir
well, heat up and season with salt and pepper and a dash of
lemon juice.

4_   Sprinkle finely chopped parsley on top.

Per serving: P: 15 g, F: 6 g, C: 30 g, kJ: 1034, kcal: 247

>>   *A little tip:* A freshly baked baguette, a dollop of yoghurt and
the soup is perfect.

Midnight tomato soup

No soup – no goodnight.

1 bunch soup vegetables
(carrot, leeks, celery)

2 small onions

1 clove garlic

5 tbsp olive oil

1 kg/2¼ lb passata or pureed
canned tomatoes

sugar, salt, pepper

7–8 leaves fresh basil

2 tbsp cream, 4 tsp green
pesto

Preparation time: **30 minutes**

1_ Wash and prepare the vegetables for the soup and chop into coarse chunks. Peel the onions and garlic and chop them as well. Heat the olive oil in a large pan. Add the chopped vegetables, onions and garlic and fry for 3–4 minutes. Add the passata, bring to the boil and simmer for 20 minutes.

2_ Season the soup with sugar, salt and pepper and add the basil leaves. Simmer for another 5 minutes. Puree finely with a hand-held blender and stir in the cream. Serve in soup plates or bowls and garnish with a spoonful of pesto which is not only delicious but also pleasing to the eye.

Per serving: P: 6 g, F: 17 g, C: 20 g, kJ: 1089, kcal: 259

>> **Another idea:** You can also serve the soup with crème fraîche instead of pesto and garnish with basil leaves.

>> **And another idea:** Simmer the soup for a few more minutes to thicken and you will have a super pasta sauce.

Pepper soup with sesame seeds and goat's cheese

There is nothing to bleat about.

750 g/1½ lb yellow sweet
peppers

2 red chilli peppers

2 onions

some olive oil

700 ml/24 fl oz (3 cups)
vegetable stock

1 dash lemon juice

salt, pepper from the mill

sugar

120 g/4 oz goat's cheese

2 tbsp sesame seeds

Preparation time: **50 minutes**

1_ Cut the peppers and chillies in half, remove the stalks and seeds as well as the white membranes. Wash the peppers and chillies and cut into fine strips.

2_ Peel the onions and chop finely. Heat the olive oil in the pan, add the chopped onions and fry until transparent. Now add the peppers and chillies and fry for a further 5 minutes. Add the stock, bring to the boil, reduce the heat, cover and simmer for 30 minutes.

3_ Puree the soup with a hand-held blender until completely smooth. Season with lemon juice, a pinch of sugar, salt and pepper. Cut the goat's cheese into 4 equally large pieces, coat in sesame seeds and place on the soup.

Per serving: P: 6 g, F: 14 g, C: 12 g, kJ: 843, kcal: 202

Good fishing

It would be a shame to have it only on Fridays.

>> They come from another world. They are major sources
of iodine, protein and omega 3 fatty acids: fresh fish
and seafood.

Their scales do not appeal to anyone. But most people love the
delicate, tender flesh and of course the flavour which comes
from the sea.
Yes, yes, but what about preparation? It's quicker and easier
than most people think, as the next few pages will show.

Fish Caprese

Italian for beginners.

>> It maybe surprising to find the mozzarella and tomatoes side by side with tender fish fillets. But anyone fishing this threesome out of the oven is extremely fortunate. What is more, it's very easy to make:

4 tomatoes

2 small courgettes

1 packet (250 g/9 oz) mozzarella

salt, pepper from the mill

1 tbsp dried Italian herbs

4 tbsp olive oil

4 pollack or rosefish fillets (about 130 g/4½ oz each)

some sprigs basil

Preparation time: **50 minutes**

1_ Wash the tomatoes and wipe them dry. Remove the stalks and cut the tomatoes into slices.

2_ Wash the courgettes and wipe dry. Cut off the ends, then cut into thin slices. Drain the mozzarella and cut into 12 slices.

3_ Arrange half the mozzarella, courgette and tomato slices in such a way that they overlap in a shallow, well greased soufflé dish. Season with salt and pepper and half the herbs and sprinkle 2 tablespoons of the olive oil on top.

4_ Rinse the fish fillets under cold water, wipe dry, season with salt and pepper and arrange on the vegetable-cheese mixture. Then arrange the rest of the tomatoes, courgettes and mozzarella.

5_ Season with salt, pepper and the remaining herbs. Sprinkle the rest of the olive oil on top. Bake the fish, uncovered, in the oven preheated to 200 °C/400 °F (Gas mark 6), fan oven 180 °C/350 °F (Gas mark 4) for 25–30 minutes.

6_ Rinse the basil, pat dry, pull the leaves off the stems, cut into thin strips and sprinkle over the fish, tomatoes, courgettes and mozzarella.

Per serving: P: 38 g, F: 27 g, C: 4 g, kJ: 1717, kcal: 410

>> *A good tip:* This is delicious served with rice or potato puree (see page 48/49). You can also use deep-frozen fish.

Fish en papillotte

It's in the bag!

>> This fish is so delicious that you'd like to wrap it as a present. In fact, wrapping the fish is a clever way of cooking it because it is easy and preserves all the aroma of the fish and herbs. You must try this:

4 zander fillets or tilapia
fillets without skin
(about 160 g/5½ oz each)

1 bunch soup vegetables
(carrot, celery, leeks)

1 small fennel bulb

1 onion

1 clove garlic

1 sprig each parsley,

basil and dill

1 lemon (untreated, unwaxed)

salt, pepper from the mill

4 tbsp butter

In addition:

1.2 m/4 ft string

4 large sheets baking

parchment

Preparation time: **40 minutes**

1_ Rinse the fish fillets under cold water and wipe dry. Wash and prepare the vegetables, peel and cut into very thin strips. Wash and prepare the fennel and cut into thin slices. Remove the green leaves of the fennel.

2_ Peel the onion and garlic and chop up finely. Wash the herbs and green fennel leaves, pat dry and pull the leaves off the stems. Wash the lemon carefully and cut off four slices of equal size. Squeeze the rest of the lemon. Sprinkle the lemon juice over the fish fillets, then season with salt and pepper.

3_ Cut the string into 8 pieces 15-cm/6-in long. Arrange the sheets of baking parchment on the baking sheet and put similar amounts of vegetables and herbs on the middle of each. Then put the fish fillet on top and garnish with 1 slice of lemon and 1 tablespoon of butter.

4_ Next pull the long sides of the baking parchment together over the fish to close the parcel and pleat together like an accordion. Twist the ends like those of a sweet wrapper and tie with the string.

5_ Bake in the oven preheated to 220 °C/425 °F (Gas mark 7), fan oven 200 °C/400 °F (Gas mark 6). Then remove from the oven, leave to rest for 5 minutes and serve.

Per serving: P: 32 g, F: 18 g, C: 7 g, kJ: 1373, kcal: 328

>> *A simple tip:* Serve with plain boiled potatoes and a crisp green salad. You can also use frozen fish.

Saint Peter's fish
with spinach and orange

Saint Peter and his retinue.

4 frozen St Peter's fish fillets

(about 160 g/5½ oz each)

300 g/10 oz frozen leaf

spinach

1 orange (untreated,

unwaxed)

salt, pepper from the mill

1–2 tbsp plain flour

3 tbsp olive oil for frying

1 carton whipping cream

Preparation time: **40 minutes**

(excluding defrosting time)

1_ Defrost the fish and leaf spinach. Rinse the fillets under cold water and wipe dry. Drain the spinach thoroughly or, even better, squeeze out all the water. Wash the orange carefully and grate the zest. Remove any remaining rind and all the white pith with a sharp knife. Separate the segments, remove the membranes and put to one side for the garnish.

2_ Cut each fish fillet into four strips: first cut through the middle lengthways, then cut each half in two lengthways. Season the strips with salt and pepper and coat in the flour. Shake off the excess flour.

3_ Heat the oil in a pan, add the strips of fish and fry briefly but briskly on both sides, then place in a greased soufflé dish. Season the spinach with salt and pepper and arrange round the fish fillets. Then sprinkle the grated orange zest on top. Finally pour the cream over the fish and spinach and bake in the oven preheated to 220 °C/425 °F (Gas mark 7), fan oven 200 °C/400 °F (Gas mark 6) for 10–12 minutes.

4_ Take the fish out of the oven. Arrange the spinach on the plates and arrange 4 strips of fish on each. Pour the sauce on top. If necessary, bring the sauce briefly to the boil for a creamier consistency. Garnish with the orange segments.

Per serving: P: 13 g, F: 25 g, C: 8 g, kJ: 1343, kcal: 321

>> **Accompaniment:** Delicious served with plain boiled potatoes.

>> **An alternative?** Instead of Saint Peter's fish, you could also used tilapia or pollack.

>> **Something easier?** If you find removing the membranes of the orange segments too fiddly, just cut them into cubes.

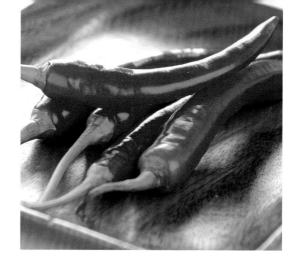

Prawns with coconut milk and chillies

The East comes into the kitchen.

>> Sweet and sour and amazingly exotic, that's how prawns should taste. Just ask around – or try this recipe:

400 ml/14 fl oz (1¾ cups) coconut milk

1 tbsp yellow chilli paste

450 g/1 lb peeled king prawns

2 tbsp fish sauce

½ tbsp sugar or honey

1–2 sprigs coriander (cilantro)

1 red chilli pepper

some lime slices

Preparation time: **20 minutes**

1_ Heat half the coconut milk in a pan or wok, add the chilli paste, stir until the mixture is beautifully smooth and simmer for 2–3 minutes until it begins to develop its aroma.

2_ Rinse the prawns, pat dry, add to the pan or wok and cook for 1 minute. Now add the rest of the coconut milk, the fish sauce and the sugar or honey. Allow to simmer for 2 minutes. Rinse the coriander, pat dry and pull the leaves off the stems. Wash the chillies, remove the stalks and cut diagonally into rings.

3_ Arrange in individual bowls or a serving dish. Garnish with the chilli rings, coriander leaves and sliced lime. Exquisite!

Per serving: P: 25 g, F: 19 g, C: 8 g, kJ: 1278, kcal: 308

>> **The perfect accompaniment:** it is ideally served with rice.

Meatily good

Delicious through and through.

>> Between ourselves: what is more human than an irresistible desire for meat? There's hardly a fantasy in the minds of cooks that does not involve beautiful shapes, golden-brown skin or perfect joints. But it should not be every day.

On the contrary: less also means better quality meat – preferably organic. Many find that it tastes much better and is much healthier. And very pleasantly so. Now let's start eating.

Mediterranean chicken wings

Recommended flight plan.

>> Just give a thought to these tasty fliers and give them permission to land on your plate. Follow the recipe for a delicious meal:

For the marinade:

1 sprig each rosemary and thyme

3–4 cloves garlic

salt

4–5 tbsp olive oil

juice of 2 lemons

24 chicken wings (1.4 kg/3 lb)

pepper from the mill

5–6 cocktail tomatoes

Preparation time: **70 minutes**

1_ For the marinade, rinse the rosemary and thyme, pat dry, and pull the leaves off the stems. Peel the garlic, squeeze through a garlic press and mix together with the herbs, a little salt and some of the olive oil. Stir in the lemon juice.

2_ Rinse the chicken wings under cold water and wipe dry, then put them in bowl and pour the marinade over them. Now add the rest of the olive oil, season with pepper, cover and leave to stand for 15–20 minutes.

3_ Now take the chicken wings out of the marinade and put on a baking sheet lined with baking parchment. Brush a little more of the marinade on the chicken wings.

4_ Put the baking sheet in the oven preheated to 180–200 °C/ 350–400 °F (Gas mark 4–6), fan oven 160–180°C/325–350 °F (Gas mark 3–4) and cook for about 45 minutes, brushing the chicken wings now and again with the remaining marinade. After 30 minutes add the washed, halved tomatoes. Serve either hot or cold.

Per serving: P: 29 g, F: 39 g, C: 2 g, kJ: 2005, kcal: 478

>> *Fancy a variation? Spicy chicken drumsticks (small photograph).* For the marinade, remove the stalk of 1 red chilli and cut into thin rings. Pour 100 ml/3½ fl oz (½ cup) chicken or vegetable stock into a pan and add 3 tablespoons ketchup, 1 tablespoon each sugar, soy sauce and vinegar and 1 teaspoon each sambal oelek and curry. Bring to the boil, stirring all the time. Take 20 drumsticks (about 1.5 kg/3¼ lb), rinse, wipe dry and place on a baking sheet lined with baking parchment. Brush the drumsticks with a generous coating of marinade and leave for 10 minutes. Then cook in the oven preheated to 180–200 °C/350–400 °F (Gas mark 4–6), fan oven 160–180°C/325–350 °F (Gas mark 3–4) as above. Brush the drumsticks with the rest of marinade during the cooking process. Serve hot or cold.

Goulash

And it's good.

For 4–6 people

300 g/10 oz onions

500 g/18 oz beef without
bones, e.g. braising steak

3 tbsp cooking oil

salt, pepper from the mill

paprika powder

2 slightly heaped tbsp
tomato puree

about 250 ml/8 fl oz (1 cup)
hot water

2–3 sweet peppers

1 red chilli pepper

1–2 dashes Tabasco sauce

Preparation time: **100 minutes**

1_ Peel the onions, cut in half and then into slices. Rinse the meat under running cold water, wipe dry and then cut into 3-cm/1¼-in cubes.

2_ Heat 2 tablespoons of the oil in a pan. Add the meat and fry until brown all over. Add the rest of the oil and the sliced onion and fry with the meat.

3_ Season the meat with salt, pepper and paprika; stir in the tomato puree. Add the hot water, cover and braise the meat over medium heat for 70–80 minutes. If necessary, add a little more water later.

4_ Cut the peppers in half, remove the stalks and the seeds. Wash and cut coarsely into cubes. Remove the stalks of the chilli and cut into slices. After about one hour add the peppers and chilli to the goulash. Stir and continue simmering. Finally season with salt, pepper, paprika powder and Tabasco.

Per serving: P: 23 g, F: 9 g, C: 6 g, kJ: 852, kcal: 204

>> **By the way:** Instead using salt, pepper and paprika powder, you could use goulash seasoning.
You can make your goulash even more sophisticated in taste by replacing half the water with red wine. Instead of beef you can also use lean pork (braising time about 45 minutes), or half beef and half pork. Goulash is also suitable for freezing.

>> **The best accompaniments:** Potatoes, noodles and rice.

>> **A variation? Goulash with mushrooms.** Replace the peppers and chillies by 200 g/7 oz mushrooms. Wash and prepare the mushrooms, cut off the ends of the stalks and any bad parts. Wipe clean or rinse and wipe dry; then cut into slices and add to the goulash 10 minutes before the end of the cooking time. Or drain 1 small jar of sliced mushroom in a sieve and add to the goulash just before the end.

>> **Another variation: Goulash soup** (photograph). Cut the meat cubes a little smaller and instead of 250 ml/8 fl oz (1 cup) water, use 500 ml/17 fl oz (2¼ cups) of beef or vegetable stock. Serve the soup with a crisp baguette.

Leg of lamb
using the 80 °C method
A big leg. But not a big deal.

>> Big cars, big houses, big animals: big things command respect. You only need a little time, a taste for extra tender lamb and you will be amazed what a magnificent meal you end up with. Such as this:

For 4–6 people

about 2 kg/4½ lb leg of lamb

10–12 small cloves garlic

1 sprig rosemary

1 sprig thyme

salt, pepper from the mill

For the marinade:

1 tbsp runny honey

1 tbsp mustard (e.g. Dijon)

2 tbsp olive oil

In addition:

2 onions

100 ml/3½ fl oz (½ cup) red wine

400 ml/14 fl oz (1¾ cups) veal stock

Preparation time: **40 minutes**

(+6½ hours cooking time)

1_ Preheat the oven to 250 °C/480 °F (Gas mark 9). Remove the sinews and the fat from the leg. Rinse under cold water and wipe dry.

2_ Peel the garlic, rinse the herbs and pat dry. Remove the leaves from the stems and chop coarsely. Then score the skin of the leg of lamb with a sharp, pointed knife 10–12 times in several places and open the cuts a little with your fingers.

3_ Sprinkle the cloves of garlic, chopped herbs and 1 teaspoon salt over the leg of lamb, rub in and press inside the cuts made by the scoring until everything has been divided evenly. Season with pepper.

4_ Make a marinade with honey, mustard and olive oil. Put the leg of lamb in a roasting tin and spread the marinade thickly all over it. Then put in the bottom third of the hot oven. If there is a grill inside your oven, turn it on and brown the leg of lamb for about 15 minutes, turning once.

5_ Switch off the grill and reduce the oven temperature to 80 °C/ 180 °F. At the same time open the oven door a little so that the oven cools down quickly. Then close the door again.

6_ Peel the onions, chop finely and add to the leg of lamb. Cook the leg of lamb for about 6 ½ hours. After 2 hours turn the leg over and add the red wine. After another 2 hours turn the leg again and add the veal stock.

Per serving: P: 71 g, F: 19 g, C: 7 g, kJ: 2076, kcal: 495

>> **Big tips:** This is delicious served with a potato gratin (page 50/51) and ratatouille (page 76/77). Or with plain boiled potatoes and green beans with savory and some freshly ground pepper.

Marinated chicken legs
with rosemary potatoes

Make your hunger walk away.

4 large chicken legs (about
200 g/7 oz each)

Classic oriental marinade
from page 24

1 chilli pepper

For the vegetables:

1 each red and yellow sweet
pepper

1 courgette

2 spring onions

2 tomatoes

1–2 tbsp olive oil

salt, pepper from the mill

For the rosemary potatoes:

1 kg/2¼ lb medium potatoes

1 sprig fresh or dried
rosemary

3 tbsp olive oil, salt

Preparation time: **45 minutes**
(excluding marinading or
cooking time)

1_ Rinse the chicken legs under cold water and wipe dry.

2_ Make the marinade following the instructions on page 24
    and brush on the chicken legs. Wash and prepare the chilli,
    cut into rings and add to the chicken and marinade. Put the
    marinating chicken in the fridge for 1–2 hours. Turn the legs
    now and again and baste with the marinade.

3_ Cut the peppers in half and remove the stalks and seeds. Cut
    out the white membranes. Wash the peppers and cut into
    chunks. Wash the courgettes, cut off the ends, cut in half
    lengthways, then cut into cubes. Wash and prepare the spring
    onions and cut into pieces 3 cm/1¼ in long. Cut the tomatoes
    in four and remove the base of the stalks. Mix together the
    peppers, courgettes, spring onions and tomatoes and stir
    some olive oil into them. Now put all the vegetables in a
    soufflé dish. Season with coarse sea salt and pepper.

4_ Arrange the chicken legs on top of the vegetables and cook
    in the oven preheated to 180 °C/350 °F (Gas mark 4), fan oven
    160 °C/325 °F (Gas mark 3) for 30–40 minutes.

5_ Peel the potatoes, rinse and cut in half. Add the rosemary,
    olive oil and salt and mix well. Place them in another gratin
    dish, put in the oven with the chicken legs and cook for about
    25 minutes. Are the chicken legs ready? Then take them out,
    season the vegetables again and serve with the rosemary
    potatoes and chicken legs. Simply first-class!

Per serving: P: 35 g, F: 31 g, C: 43 g, kJ: 2509, kcal: 559

>> *By the way:* Both gratin dishes must be of a size that they will
    fit next to each other in the oven.

Saltimbocca alla romana

Veal escalope Roman-style.

>> "Salt'im bocca!" is an old Roman saying which means something like "Jump in the mouth". If your saltimbocca does not perform as requested in this way, just use your knife and fork. It will taste delicious anyway.

4 thin slices veal from the leg
(100 g/3½ oz each)

8 leaves sage

4 slices Parma ham

salt, pepper from the mill

20 g/¾ oz plain flour

2–3 tbsp cooking oil

wooden cocktail sticks

For the sauce:

125 ml/4 fl oz (½ cup) white wine

125 g/4½ oz double cream

salt, pepper, sugar

Preparation time: **30 minutes**

1_ Rinse the slices of veal and the sage leaves under cold water, wipe or dab dry. Cut the slices of veal and Parma ham in half. Place 1 half slice of Parma ham on each half-slice of veal and garnish with 1 sage leaf. Secure by inserting a wooden cocktail stick from the top. Season with salt and pepper on both sides and coat in flour on both sides.

2_ Heat the oil in a pan, add the meat and fry on each side for 3–4 minutes. Arrange on plates warmed beforehand and covered with a second plate.

3_ For the sauce, add white wine to the cooking juices in the pan and reduce a little. Add the double cream, heat up briefly and season with salt, pepper and sugar. Stir in the meat juices and pour the sauce over the meat.

Per serving: P: 25 g, F: 22 g, C: 4 g, kJ: 1388, kcal: 334

>> **You have no veal?** Pork or turkey fillet will also do.

>> **Best accompaniment:** Pasta or rice.

>> **A little tip:** You could use mascarpone instead of double cream.

Saté kebabs with peanut sauce

Popular with all and sundry.

For 4–6 people

For the kebabs:

4 chicken breast fillets
(about 160 g/5½ oz each)

2 cloves garlic

1 small onion

1 red chilli pepper

1 large pinch cumin

2 tbsp light soy sauce

500 ml/17 fl oz (2¼ cups)
coconut milk

2 tbsp cooking oil

salt, pepper from the mill

For the peanut sauce:

1 small packet (100 g/3½ oz)
salted peanuts

1 lemon (untreated, unwaxed)

2 tbsp peanut butter

1 tsp curry powder

1 pinch sugar

3–5 tbsp cream

In addition:

8–10 sticks lemon grass

Preparation time: **40 minutes**
(excluding marinating time)

1_ Rinse the chicken fillets under cold water, wipe dry and cut into short strips 1.25–2 cm/½–¾ in wide. Peel the onions and garlic and chop as finely as possible. Wash the chilli, cut in half lengthways, remove the stalks and seeds and cut into thin strips.

2_ Mix together the garlic, onion, chilli, cumin, soy sauce, 4 tablespoons coconut milk and the oil and stir to incorporate all the ingredients. Season with salt and pepper. Leave the strips of chicken breasts to marinate for 1–2 hours.

3_ Meanwhile roast the peanuts in a pan without fat, leave to cool and chop finely or crush. Wash the lemon in hot water, wipe dry and grate the rind. Squeeze the rest of the lemon. Add the remaining coconut milk, peanut butter and curry powder to the pan and bring to the boil. Stir in the crushed or chopped peanuts, grated lemon zest and lemon juice, a pinch of sugar and enough cream to make it deliciously creamy.

4_ Allow the pieces of meat to drain briefly and thread onto the stems of lemon grass in a wave-like shape. You can cut off the thick end of the lemon grass and freeze to use another time. Place the kebabs a little distance from each other under the preheated grill, brushing them with the marinade now and again. No grill? No problem, just fry the kebabs in a pan in a little oil. Serve with the peanut sauce.

Per serving: P: 40 g/1½ oz, F: 39 g, C: 8 g, kJ: 2239, kcal: 539

>> **Somethings else?** You can also make these saté kebabs with strips of pork fillet or beef fillet. But in that case it is best to make the holes in the meat first with a wooden skewer. And you can also use wooden skewers instead of lemon grass.

Breaded pork escalopes

Quite mouthwatering.

>> There are times when a fried breadcrumb coating makes all the difference and when such a veal cutlet is presented on a plate, it is irresistible. Here's the recipe:

4 pork escalopes (about
200 g/7 oz each)

salt, pepper from the mill

2 tbsp plain flour

2 eggs

3 tbsp breadcrumbs

5 tbsp cooking oil

Preparation time: **20 minutes**

1_ Season the pork escalopes with salt and pepper. Put three plates next to each other – one with the flour, one with the eggs and one with the breadcrumbs. Roll the escalopes in the flour and shake off the excess. Beat the eggs in a soup plate until foamy, using a fork. Roll the floured escalopes first in the beaten egg, then in the breadcrumbs.

2_ Heat the oil in a pan until very hot. Add the escalopes and fry briskly on both sides, then continue frying over medium heat for 3–5 minutes, depending on the thickness, until done. Turn over now and again. Take the escalopes out of the pan.

Per serving: P: 47 g, F: 15 g, C: 6 g, kJ: 1471, kcal: 351

>> **Try the dish with these accompaniments:** A slice of lemon, French fries or roast potatoes, following the recipe on page 56/57, and a green salad.

>> **Another tip:** So that they remain nice and airy, do not press the breadcrumbs too hard.

>> **Fancy a schnitzel "chasseur"?** Peel and chop 1 onion. Wash and prepare 250 g/9 oz mushrooms, wipe clean with kitchen paper or rinse and wipe dry, then cut into slices. Prepare the escalopes as above, coat in breadcrumbs and fry. Cover and keep in warm place. Add the chopped onion to the cooking fat in the pan and fry. Now add the sliced mushrooms and fry with the chopped onion. Season with salt and pepper and fry gently over low heat for 2–3 minutes without a lid. Now stir in a tub of crème fraîche and 1 tablespoon of parsley. Serve the escalope with this sauce or the mushroom sauce described on page 152/153.

Fillet steak

Good meat is never too good.

4 tbsp cooking oil

4 beef fillet steaks from
the middle of the fillet

(150 g/5 oz each)

salt, pepper from the mill

Preparation time: **10 minutes**

1_ Heat the oil in a pan until very hot. Fry the steaks briskly on both sides. Then fry 2–3 minutes on each side, basting often with the meat juices. Season with salt and pepper.

2_ Put the steaks on pre-warmed plates and pour the cooking juices over the steaks.

Per serving: P: 32 g, F: 16 g, C: 0 g, kJ: 1128, kcal: 269

>> **Accompaniment:** French fries and a mixed green salad or the potato gratin from pages 50/51.

>> **To make it even more perfect:** Leave the meat to rest a little after frying so that the meat juices become distributed throughout and the steak remains tasty and tender. Pour any meat juices which emerge back onto the steaks or use to make the sauce. The 3-minute steak ("medium") is particularly popular, being somewhere between near-raw ("rare", 1–2 minutes) and cooked through ("well done", 5 minutes). The frying times indicated refer to one side only.

Rump steaks with onions

When vegetarians might become tempted.

2 large onions

4 rump steaks (200 g/7 oz
each)

3 tbsp cooking oil

salt, pepper from the mill

steak seasoning (optional)

Preparation time: **20 minutes**

1_ Peel the onions and cut into slices. Make a few cuts in the edges of the steaks.

2_ Heat the oil in a pan until very hot. Add the meat to the hot fat in the pan and fry briskly on both sides. Season with salt and pepper (and steak seasoning if you like), then fry for 3–4 minutes on each side. Baste the steaks frequently with the meat juices in the pan so that they remain juicy.

3_ Put the steaks on a pre-warmed serving dish, cover and keep in a warm place. Add the onion slices to the pan and fry. Season with salt and pepper and fry for a few minutes until golden brown, stirring all the time. Serve the steaks with the onions.

Per serving: P: 45 g, F: 16 g, C: 1 g, kJ: 1399, kcal: 333

>> **These accompaniments will complete the dish:** Potato wedges (page 52/53) and green beans or mixed salad.

Puddings

Now: your just desserts!

>> It's only after you have finished your main course that
the real eating starts, in the shape of a pudding, sweet or
dessert. Don't feel guilty about the puddings you like – you
deserve a reward!

Sometimes it seems as if there is not enough time to make
this the "highlight" of the meal. But these recipes are really
easy to make, as you will see in the following pages.

Rice pudding

Also tasty with chopsticks.

>> This rice pudding is pure delight – every single grain of it. Just imagine how much pleasure that will be in one serving which contains hundreds of grains! Meanwhile try the following:

For 4–6 people:

1 litre/1¾ pints (4½ cups) milk

1 pinch salt

2–3 tbsp sugar

1 tbsp finely grated lemon zest

175 g/6 oz (¾ cup) pudding rice (short grain)

Preparation time: **40 minutes**

1_ Rinse a pan under cold water but do not dry it; this will prevent the milk from burning on the bottom of the pan. Bring the milk to the boil with the salt, sugar and lemon zest.

2_ Add the pudding rice, stir and bring to the boil again. Leave to simmer for about 35 minutes with the lid half on, stirring now and again.

3_ Serve the rice pudding hot or cold.

Per serving: P: 8 g, F: 6 g, C: 43 g, kJ: 1189, kcal: 285

>> **Little tip:** Serve the rice pudding as a main course with brown butter and cinnamon sugar, stewed fruit or fresh fruit.

>> **Fancy a variation?** Roast 40 g/1½ oz (¼ cup) flaked almonds or hazelnuts in a pan without fat. Sprinkle them over the rice and pour some maple syrup or honey on top.

Apple tart with almonds

Picked from the gourmets' family tree.

>> Apple tart has close family connections with Alsace, the land of gourmets. Puff pastry is also part of the family. Although it sometimes comes with ham and cheese, sweet tarts have the last word here. This is how you make one:

For 6 people:

½ packet (225 g/8 oz) frozen puff pastry

2 tasty apples (sweet and sour, e.g. Cox's orange)

1 packet finely chopped lemon zest

1 packet Bourbon vanilla sugar

2 tbsp sugar

125 ml/4 fl oz (½ cup) whipping cream

2 eggs

1 handful slivered almonds

1 tbsp icing sugar

Preparation time: **40 minutes**

1_ Defrost the puff pastry, following the instructions on the packet. Then arrange the sheets on top of each but do not knead them! Roll out to obtain a sheet with a diameter of about 32 cm/12½ in. Then take a springform mould 26–28 cm/10–11 in in diameter, rinsed in cold water (and not dried), and arrange the pastry so that it reaches over the edge slightly.

2_ Remove the core of the apple with a round apple-corer. Peel it and cut it into thin slices with the hole in the middle. Arrange the apple slices on the puff pastry so that they overlap.

3_ Mix the lemon zest, Bourbon vanilla sugar, sugar, cream and eggs and whisk to incorporate. Pour this mixture over the apple slices and bake for 20 minutes in the oven preheated to 200 °C/400 °F (Gas mark 6), fan oven 180 °C/350 °F (Gas mark 4).

4_ Let the tart cool a little after taking it out of the oven and cut off the pastry projecting over the edge. Carefully loosen it from the mould, sprinkle generously with icing sugar and serve lukewarm.

Per serving: P: 6 g, F: 20 g, C: 25 g, kJ: 1287, kcal: 308

>> **Tip:** Instead of rolling it out yourself, you can buy round sheets of puff pastry (about 225 g/8 oz, diameter 32 cm/12 ½ in). Just line the springform mould with one, letting some of it project beyond the edge (if necessary roll it out a little more).

>> **Tip number 2:** if you do not have a round apple corer you can cut the apple in two, remove the core with a knife and then cut the two apple halves into slices.

Orange pannacotta
with rum

Whoever starts first is the loser.

600 ml/21 oz (2½ cups)
whipping cream

2–3 drops vanilla essence

1 pinch salt

1 tbsp grated lemon zest

3–4 tbsp sugar

1 orange (untreated,
unwaxed)

4 sheets clear gelatine

3 tbsp rum

For the sauce:

some orange juice

1–2 tbsp sugar

Preparation time: **40 minutes**
(excluding cooling time)

1_ Rinse a pan in cold water. Mix together the cream, Bourbon vanilla essence, salt, lemon zest and sugar. Bring to the boil and simmer over low heat for about 10 minutes without a lid. Wash the orange carefully, wipe dry, and grate the rind thinly. Add the grated orange rind to the cream mixture 3–4 minutes before the end of the cooking time and simmer briefly.

2_ Soak the gelatine as instructed on the packet. Remove the pan from the heat. Squeeze the gelatine and dissolve in the hot cream mixture while stirring. Add the rum. Take 4 ramekins or cups, each of about 150 ml/5 fl oz (generous ½ cup), rinsed out with cold water. Pour in the cream, then leave to cool a little and refrigerate for at least 3 hours or, even better, overnight.

3_ Remove the rest of the orange rind together with all the white pith, using a sharp knife. Remove the orange segments without the membrane. Squeeze the rest of the orange and top up with orange juice to make 200 ml/7 fl oz (scant cup). Pour into a pan with sugar and reduce to make a slightly thick syrup, then refrigerate.

4_ Loosen the pannacotta round the edge with a knife, place each ramekin in hot water for a few seconds, then turn out onto a dessert plate. Pour the sauce over the top and decorate with the orange segments.

Per serving: P: 5 g, F: 47 g, C: 32 g, kJ: 2560, kcal: 612

>> *A little tip:* Instead of orange segments, you could also use tinned mandarin oranges. In this case, squeeze the orange and use the juice to make the sauce.

>> *Try something different? Pannacotta with berry sauce.* Prepare the pannacotta as described in the recipe but leave out the grated orange rind. For the berry sauce, puree 300 g/10 oz strawberries, raspberries or frozen mixed berries and stir in a sachet of Bourbon vanilla sugar.

>> *Another variation: Pannacotta with yoghurt.* Prepare as usual but with only 350 g/12 oz of cream. After stirring in the gelatine, stir in 250 g/9 oz of yoghurt or vanilla yoghurt. Continue as above.

Chocolate mousse

A must for chocolate lovers.

>> The Olmecs, an ancient people who lived in the lowlands of south-central Mexico, already knew that the cocoa plant was divine some 3,500 years ago. And they were right. Today very few sweet foods are more popular than chocolate. It is exciting, versatile and irresistible, as in this recipe:

For 6 people:

375 g/13 oz dark chocolate

2 fresh eggs

2 fresh egg yolks

500 ml/17 fl oz (2¼ cups) whipping cream

3 tbsp cognac or crème de cacao (chocolate liqueur)

Preparation time: **25 minutes** (excluding cooling time)

1_ Chop the chocolate into small pieces and put in a bowl. Put this bowl in a pan with very hot but not boiling water (bain-marie), so that the chocolate melts. Stir occasionally. Then leave to cool.

2_ Whisk the eggs and egg yolks with a hand-held mixer until the mixture becomes creamy. Whip the cream stiff and stir into the egg mixture. Then carefully fold the melted, cooled chocolate into the egg-cream mixture. Stir very gently so that the air in the mixture does not escape. Flavour with cognac or crème de cacao.

3_ Put the mousse in bowls, cups or a pretty serving bowl and refrigerate for 1–2 hours. Enjoy it on its own or with some delicious summer berries. Exquisite!

Per serving: P: 9 g, F: 51 g, C: 36 g, kJ: 2755, kcal: 661

>> *A little tip:* To give the mousse a devilish note, add a small washed, prepared and finely chopped chilli to the chocolate as it melts in the bain-marie. Or add 2–3 dashes of Tabasco.

>> *Important:* Because of the raw eggs it contains, the chocolate must be kept in the refrigerator and eaten the same day.

Strawberry hill

An expedition to the highest peak of pleasure.

>> Are you prepared for a sweet adventure? In order to climb these delicious heights you only need a spoon. The only danger is that you might want more!

For 6 people:

500 g/18 oz fresh

strawberries

4 tbsp sugar

juice of 1 lemon

½ packet shortbread or

cookies

2 packets custard powder,

vanilla flavour

100 g/3½ oz (scant 1½ cups)

sugar

500 ml/17 fl oz (2¼ cups)

milk

500 ml/17 fl oz (2¼ cups)

whipping cream

Preparation time: **30 minutes**

1_ Wash the strawberries and keep six of the best-looking ones for the garnish. Remove the stalks of the other strawberries, cut into quarters, sprinkle the sugar on top and leave to stand in the lemon juice for 10–15 minutes.

2_ Meanwhile line 6 pudding bowls or a glass serving bowl with biscuits. Prepare the vanilla pudding with the sugar and the amount of milk and whipping cream indicated in this recipe, following the instructions on the packet.

3_ First arrange a layer of marinated strawberries on the biscuits, then pour the still warm vanilla pudding over the strawberries and biscuits. Decorate with the whole strawberries you put aside and refrigerate.

Per serving: P: 7 g, F: 32 g, C: 58 g, KJ: 2401, kcal: 573

>> *A little tip:* If you like you can also marinate the strawberries in Cointreau or Grand Marnier (orange liqueur).

>> *Another tip:* If you are in a rush you can always use ready-made custard (2 tubs of 500 g/18 oz each).

>> *And another tip:* Defrosted mixed berries can also be used instead of strawberries.

Quick cheesecake

More taste, more speed.

Makes 12 servings:

200 g/7 oz (1 cup) butter

6 eggs

250 g/9 oz (1 cup) sugar

1 packet vanilla sugar

1 tbsp grated lemon zest

2–3 tbsp lemon juice

1 kg/2¼ lb curd cheese

2 packets custard powder, vanilla flavour

1 level tsp baking powder

some breadcrumbs

Preparation time: **20 minutes** (excluding baking or cooling time)

1_ Take the butter and eggs out of the refrigerator at least 1 hour before using. This will ensure they bind better and that the mixture will not curdle. Whisk together the butter, sugar and vanilla sugar with a hand-held mixer with whisk attachment until the sugar has melted and the butter is lighter in colour. Add the eggs one by one, continuing to whisk vigorously.

2_ Mix together the grated lemon zest and juice with the curd cheese, then stir into the butter and egg mixture. Mix together the custard powder and baking powder, sieve and stir in. Grease a 26–28-cm/10–11-in springform mould and sprinkle breadcrumbs on the bottom; this will make it easier to remove from the mould afterwards. Now spoon the mixture into it.

3_ Bake in the oven preheated to 180 °C/350 °F (Gas mark 4), fan oven 160 °C/325 °F (Gas mark 3) for about 60 minutes. Then turn off the oven but leave the cheesecake inside and open the oven door slightly. Take the cheesecake out when the oven has cooled down and remove it from the mould.

Per serving: P: 14 g, F: 21 g, C: 29 g, kJ: 1565, kcal: 374

>> **Tip:** You can also add 50 g/2 oz raisins to the curd cheese mixture.

>> **Another tip:** When using an old baking tin it is best to line it with baking parchment to avoid it imparting any off-flavour.

>> **And another tip:** The curd cheese mixture can be divided into several small individual baking tins or muffin tins and baked for 20–30 minutes, depending on the size of the tins. It is even nicer served with ricotta, a little honey and fresh berries.

Basics

If you've got them, you've got taste.

>> It is always the largest item on the plate which attracts the most attention. But in reality it is the smaller items at the sides which are often the most rewarding: sophisticated sauces, pastes, creams, dips or vinaigrettes.

They are modest and often you will only need a small amount for new gustatory worlds to open up before you. And if you think you have to be an experienced chef to prepare these delicious sauces and dips, you only need to read these pages to realise you are wrong.

Tsatsiki

The Greeks made it easy.

>> The Greeks would never have invented philosophy or democracy with a heavy meal inside them. They must have had something light up their sleeve. Maybe it was this tsatsiki:

150 g/5 oz cucumber

2 cloves garlic

300 g/10 oz yoghurt

(preferably Greek)

salt, pepper from the mill

Preparation time: **15 minutes**

1_ Peel the cucumber, cut it in half lengthways, scoop out the seeds with a spoon and grate the cucumber finely. Peel the garlic and push through a garlic press.

2_ Stir the yoghurt to obtain a smooth consistency, then stir in the cucumber and garlic.

3_ Put the tsatsiki in the fridge and leave to stand so that the flavours will develop. Then season with salt and pepper.

In all: P: 10 g, F: 9 g, C: 14 g, kJ: 926, kcal: 222

>> *For a creamier tsatsiki:* Add 1 tablespoon each low-fat curd cheese and soured cream.

Rouille

Small dollops, big effect.

1 red sweet pepper

1 tbsp olive oil

2 small chilli peppers

salt

1 clove garlic

1 tbsp breadcrumbs

250 g/9 oz mayonnaise

Preparation time: **30 minutes**

1_ Cut the pepper in half, remove the stalks and seeds and cut into chunks. Fry the pepper for 2–3 minutes in a little oil in the pan until soft.

2_ Remove the stalks of the chillies, cut into pieces and puree with the pepper, salt and peeled garlic using the hand-held mixer until you obtain a smooth paste. Stir this paste with the breadcrumbs into the mayonnaise.

In all: P: 8 g, F: 217 g, C: 28 g, kJ: 8669, kcal: 2070

>> *Tip:* ideal with grilled meat or fish.

>> *A little variation:* Instead of red chillies you can use hot red chilli paste. Rouille should always be prepared afresh. If stored for too long, it can taste peculiar because of the garlic.

Aioli

It can still speak for itself the morning after.

4–6 cloves garlic	1_ Peel the garlic and push through a garlic press.
250 g/9 oz mayonnaise	2_ Add the garlic to the mayonnaise and stir well. Season with salt and lemon juice and leave to stand for a while.
salt	
juice of ½ lemon	In all: P: 4 g, F: 206 g, C: 8 g, kJ: 7872, kcal: 1880
Preparation time: **10 minutes**	>> ***A little tip:*** You can add a little heat to the aioli by adding some cayenne pepper. Delicious served with potato wedges, see recipe on page 52/53.

Lime, chilli and herb butters

It's never boring to eat.

750 g/1½ lb (3½ cups) soft
butter

salt, pepper from the mill

For the lime butter:

grated zest and juice of one
lime (untreated, unwaxed)

For the chilli butter:

2 red chilli peppers

or 1 tsp chilli paste

For the herb butter:

1 small onion

3 cloves garlic

5 tbsp finely chopped parsley

2–3 tbsp finely chopped
tarragon

2–3 tbsp finely chopped
chervil

7–8 finely chopped mint
leaves

5 tbsp white wine

some sugar or honey

clingfilm and aluminium foil

Preparation time: **30 minutes**

1_ Whisk all the butter with a hand-held mixer with whisk attachment until foamy and lighter in colour, when it will have almost doubled in volume. Season the butter with salt and pepper and divide into three equal portions.

2_ Add the grated zest and juice of a lime to one portion of butter and mix well.

3_ Add the chopped chillies – with the stalks removed – or chilli paste to the second portion and stir well.

4_ For the last portion of butter, peel the onions and garlic and chop finely. Add finely chopped herbs, garlic, onions, white wine and a generous pinch of sugar or honey to the butter. Whisk with the hand-held mixer on the medium setting.

5_ Shape the different butter mixtures into three long sausage shapes. Put a piece of clingfilm 30 cm/12 in long underneath each one, then wrap up and seal the ends like a sweet to form a smooth, even, firm sausage shape. Finally wrap in silver foil and again twist the ends like a sweet.

6_ Refrigerate or freeze the flavoured butter, depending on when you want to use it.

In all (lime butter): P: 0 g, F: 208 g, C: 9 g, kJ: 8085, kcal: 1932
In all (chilli butter): P: 1 g, F: 208 g, C: 2 g, kJ: 7902, kcal: 1889
In all (herb butter): P: 3 g, F: 208 g, C: 12 g, kJ: 8311, kcal: 1984

>> **By the way:** These various types of flavoured butter are a perfect accompaniment to barbecues. If there is no sauce with the fish or flash-fried meat, put some herb butter on the fish or meat while it is still hot and the butter mixture will develop into a delicious aromatic sauce.

>> **Tip:** You can also vary the herbs used in these recipes.

Yoghurt dressing

Go lightly.

For 1 salad:

300 g/10 oz yoghurt

juice of 1 lemon

sugar, salt, pepper from the

mill

some sprigs lemon balm

Preparation time: **5–10 minutes**

1_ Mix together the yoghurt and lemon juice in a bowl and season with sugar, salt and pepper.

2_ Rinse the lemon balm, pat dry, pull the leaves off the stems, chop finely and add to the yoghurt mixture.

In all: P: 9 g, F: 8 g, C: 18 g, kj: 1030, kcal: 247

>> **Tip:** Yoghurt dressing is particularly good with a plain green salad.

Herb vinaigrette

Anyone can make it.

>> Herbs mostly appear as tiny green dots. But it is worth taking a closer look at these botanical wonders. And you will realise that you too must have your own herb garden! Because it is the herbs which provide the flavour.

For 1 salad:

½ tsp medium mustard

2 tbsp lemon juice

salt, pepper from the mill

1 pinch sugar

100 ml/3½ fl oz (½ cup) olive oil

3–4 cloves garlic

1 small box cress or 1 bunch parsley

Preparation time: **10 minutes**

1_ Whisk together the mustard, lemon juice, salt, pepper and sugar and oil with a hand whisk.

2_ Peel the garlic and chop up finely. Rinse the herbs, pat dry, pull the leaves off the stems, cut the cress, chop all finely and stir into the sauce with the garlic.

In all: P: 1 g, F: 100 g, C: 5 g, kJ: 2825, kcal: 914

___

>> *A variation? The classic vinaigrette.* Chop 1 onion very finely and mix together with 1 tablespoon parsley, 1 heaped teaspoon medium-strong mustard, 3 tablespoons dark balsamic vinegar, salt and pepper. Whisk in 100 ml/3½ fl oz (½ cup) olive oil. This vinaigrette will pep up any ordinary salad such as, for instance, rocket, lamb's lettuce and cocktail tomatoes.

Thousand-island dressing

It will turn a green salad into a dream island.

For 1 salad:

250 g/9 oz mayonnaise

100 ml/3½ fl oz (½ cup) tomato ketchup

1 tsp curd cheese

½ tsp horseradish sauce

1 sprig parsley

1 tsp cognac

1 dash Tabasco

1 pinch sambal oelek

3 tbsp finely chopped mixed coloured peppers

1 dash lemon juice, salt

Preparation time: **20 minutes**

1_ Mix together the mayonnaise, ketchup, curd cheese and horseradish in a bowl. Rinse the parsley, pat dry, pull the leaves off the stems, chop up finely and stir in.

2_ Add the remaining ingredients and season the sauce with lemon juice and salt.

In all: P: 5 g, F: 132 g, C: 38 g, kJ: 5666, kcal: 1353

>> *By the way:* This is fantastic with green and mixed salads.

Red wine sauce

The essence of grapes.

400 g/14 oz onions

80 g/3 oz (6 tbsp) butter

1 litre/1¾ pints (4½ cups) red wine

1.2 litre/2 pints (5½ cups) veal stock from jar or can

1 small sprig thyme

1–2 tsp cornflour

1–2 tbsp port

salt, pepper from the mill

40 g/1½ oz cold butter

Preparation time:

40 minutes

1_ Peel the onions and chop up coarsely. Put the butter in a pan, add the onions and fry until golden yellow. Pour in the red wine and reduce to two-thirds over medium heat.

2_ Now add the veal stock and thyme sprigs and reduce to half. Remove the sprigs of thyme from the sauce, puree the sauce until completely smooth. Bring to the boil again briefly. Stir the cornflour into the port and then stir the cornflour-port mixture into the sauce. Bring to the boil again while stirring. Remove the sauce from the heat.

3_ Season the sauce with salt and pepper. Now stir in the cold butter, cut up into cubes, and whisk until the butter has melted. This will give the sauce a silky sheen and a very delicate taste.

In all: P: 16 g, F: 102 g, C: 57 g, kJ: 7517, kcal: 1794

>> *A little tip:* This is perfect with all dark and flash-fried types of meat and it is suitable for freezing.

Madeira sauce

Every dollop is an island of delight.

30 g/1 oz sugar

6–8 tbsp sherry vinegar

100 ml/3½ fl oz (½ cup) red wine

250 ml/8 fl oz (1 cup) Madeira

1 litre/1¾ pints (4½ cups) veal stock

1 bay leaf

1 sprig thyme

5 pepper corns

1–2 tsp cornflour

salt, pepper from the mill

40 g/1½ oz cold butter

Preparation time: **30 minutes**

1_ Heat the sugar in a pan until it is dissolved and has turned a golden yellow colour – in other words, caramelised. Now add the sherry vinegar – but careful, the sugar is hot! Then add the red wine and half the Madeira and reduce to half over medium heat. Stir in the veal stock, bay leaf, sprig of thyme and pepper corner and reduce again to two-thirds.

2_ Pour through a fine sieve and then return the sauce to the pan. Stir a little cornflour into the rest of the Madeira and add to the sauce to thicken. Finally remove the sauce from the heat, season with salt and pepper and stir in the cold butter.

In all: P: 9 g, F: 34 g, C: 69 g, kJ: 4215, kcal: 1007

>> *Little tip:* This is delicious with steak or fried calf's liver or chicken livers. It is also suitable for freezing.

Mushroom and cream sauce

When woodlanders give their best.

For 4–6 people:

1 onion

1 clove garlic

150 g/5 oz mushrooms

2 spring onions

1 small chilli pepper

50 g/2 oz (4 tbsp) butter

salt, pepper from the mill

400 ml/14 fl oz (1¾ cups) veal stock

500 ml/17 fl oz (2¼ cups) whipping cream

1 dash lemon juice

2 tbsp finely chopped parsley

Preparation time: **40 minutes**

1_ Peel the onion and garlic and chop finely. Prepare the mushrooms, wipe clean with kitchen paper and slice thinly. Wash and prepare the spring onions and cut into thin rings. Remove the stalk of the chilli and also cut into thin rings.

2_ Melt the butter in a large pan, add the onion and garlic and fry. Then add the slices mushrooms and continue frying. Finally add the spring onions and chillies to the pan.

3_ Season with salt and pepper, add the veal stock and reduce to half over medium heat. Now add the cream and reduce again to half. Season the sauce again with salt, pepper and lemon juice and stir in the chopped parsley.

Per serving: P: 4 g, F: 33 g, C: 5 g, kJ: 1428, kcal: 342

>> **A few ideas:** This sauce is ideal for serving with fried white meat such as pork, veal and poultry. It is particularly delicious served with bread dumplings. By boiling 600-700 g/1¼-1½ lb pasta you suddenly have mouthwatering spaghetti funghi for 4–6 people.

Quick Italian cream sauce

Speedy and delicious.

For 2–3 people:

250 ml/8 fl oz (1 cup) whipping cream

1 walnut-sized piece butter

2 sprigs basil

40 g/1½ oz (½ cup) freshly grated Parmesan

salt, pepper from the mill

ground nutmeg

Preparation time: **10 minutes**

1_ Bring the cream to the boil together with the butter in a pan. Rinse the basil, leave to drain, pull the leaves off the stems and chop finely.

2_ Stir the basil and Parmesan into the cream and season the sauce with salt, pepper and nutmeg.

Per serving: P: 7 g, F: 36 g, C: 3 g, kJ: 1525, kcal: 365

>> **A few tips:** Serve the cream sauce with 300 g/10 oz spaghetti – this is enough for 2–3 people. Stir the spaghetti into the sauce at the very last minute or it will become mushy. And: the spaghetti must not swim in the sauce but should be lightly coated with it. Always use freshly grated Parmesan. Once it has been grated it loses its aroma after a while. You can also use fresh sage instead of basil.

Any questions?

Knowledge with taste.

>> Don't worry, you won't be bombarded with complicated technical terms. Just a few pieces of practical background information which will bring light into the darkness of the kitchen. Or do you know everything about:

80 °C method: Slow cooking of large pieces of meat – this is what makes meat particularly tender. But first you must brown the meat briskly, after which the meat is roasted in the oven for 2–8 hours depending on its weight. Another advantage of this method is that the meat can be left half-an-hour longer in the oven without running the risk of drying out, for instance, when guests are a little late.

Browning or searing: Meat such as steak, for instance, is seared over high heat. This means that the oil in the pan or wok must be very hot before the meat is added.

Chillies: Only the stalk of chillies is always removed while the seeds may be left inside because that is what gives the food the required heat. If you want less heat – just remove the seeds. Very important: always wash your hands after handling chillies. If you are in a rush you can use ½ teaspoon of sambal oelek instead.

Evaporation: This is what is done with potatoes after boiling to stop them from getting mushy. After draining them, put a cloth over the pan of potatoes and return it briefly to the cooker – which has been turned off but is still hot – so as to allow any remaining liquid to evaporate as steam.

Folding in: To prevent beaten egg mixtures or whipped cream collapsing, ingredients added to them must be stirred in very carefully and gently.

Herbs: Today fresh herbs are available in almost any supermarket. In summer the range on offer is particularly great. Alternatively you can use frozen herbs or dried herbs from a packet or jar, but be sparing when using them and always make sure you check the food again after seasoning.

Number of servings indicated in the recipes: Unless otherwise stated, the quantities are always for 4 people.

Oil for cooking and frying: For frying you need oil which can be heated to a high temperature. Olive oil can be used for this purpose, as can other vegetable oils such as sunflower oil or corn oil. Clarified butter can also be used for frying; it adds a particularly delicate taste. Butter is best used only for sweating because it cannot be heated to a very high temperature. For salads you can use any cold-pressed oil.

Pinch: A pinch indicates the amount of the substance (such as salt or a spice) that you can hold between your thumb and forefinger.

Reducing sauces: By reducing sauces you increase the intensity of their taste. To reduce a sauce you allow it to cook over medium to high heat without a lid, stirring occasionally, until the sauce has thickened and the quantity has been reduced.

Sambal oelek: A very hot oriental chilli paste which must be used very sparingly because of its intense heat.

Seasoning: Very important – always taste the soup, sauce or dish with a spoon before and after adding the seasoning to make sure that the right amount of salt, pepper, heat (Tabasco, sambal oelek) or sugar is added.

Soy sauce: The perfect condiment for seasoning oriental dishes. We recommend using light soy sauce. It is also quite dark in colour but it does not make the food as dark as traditional soy sauce.

Sweating: Onions and garlic as well as other vegetables are sweated, that is, fried over medium heat in a little fat or water until transparent but not browned, stirring occasionally.

Thickening sauces: A little cornflour is stirred into water or any other cold liquid and then very slowly poured into the sauce which is to be thickened while stirring all the time.

Index from A–Z

Index from A–Z